I Pray The Lord My Soul to Keep

Edward Vaughn

WORKBOOK PRESS LLC
187 E Warm Springs Rd,
Suite B285, Las Vegas, NV 89119, USA

Website: https://workbookpress.com/
Hotline: 1-888-818-4856
Email: admin@workbookpress.com

Ordering Information:
Quantity sales. Special discounts are available on quantity purchases by corporations, associations, and others.
For details, contact the publisher at the address above.

Library of Congress Control Number:
ISBN-13:   978-1-954753-81-5 (Paperback Version)
                978-1-954753-82-2 (Digital Version)

REV. DATE: 26/03/2021

Contents

Dedication

This story is dedicated to the memory of many wonderful people who touched my life at various times during our temporary mortal lives together, and have since passed on to the eternal one. They include my beloved parents, Edward Vaughn, Sr. and Ruth Martin; my stepfather, Dr. Eric Martin; my stepmother, Eunice Vaughn; my grandparents, Alton and Lottie Vaughn, and John and Leila Dickson; my great-aunts, Janie and Annie Vaughn, and Margaret Davis; my former mother-in-law, Agnes Wilkerson; my former fathers-in-law, Steadman Humphrey and Edwin Wilkerson; my aunts, Margaret Moore, Gilbert Vaughn, and Virginia Williford; my uncles, Arthur Vaughn, Sumter Moore, and Edgar Williford; my cousins, Nancy Burns and Peggy Liles; my former brothers-in-law, Nolan Clark and John Ploeger; my closest friend from childhood, Dr. Jean LaBorde; my wise and sweet centurion friend, Mary Gardner; my old friend and boss, Roy Speer; my friend, James McArthur and his mom, Helen Hayes; My funny friend, Rue McClannahan; Russ Hinote's dear wife, Suzanne; Todd Lecka's dear wife, June; Annette's dear husband, John Spiesberger, III; Terri Union's dear husband, Carlos; Suzanne and Alyssa's dear mother, Stephanie Ploeger; my close friend and former pastor, Rev. Ben Gerardy; my brave comrades in arms who gave their mortal lives in the defense of our country, and the many other relationships with the faithful departed which have touched my life in meaningful ways. From the writing of this story, I am confident as to where all of these good folks are now, and I look forward to seeing them all again one day…and not very far down the road!

Thank You

A very special thanks to the following good people for their encouragement, helpful suggestions, and/or contributions:

John DeBoer, M.D.

Bruce Jaufman, M.D.

Wayne Riggins, M.D.

Warren McDonald, Ph.D.

Elizabeth Dean, R.N.

Malcolm King, P.E.

The Rev. Robert Alves

Rev. Bennett Gerardy +

Mary Gerardy, Ph.D.

Katherine Goodman

Bill Kirby, Jr.

Eleanor Manning

Christopher Russell

Cadet Sarah Scully

David Vaughn

Ruthi Seward, Editor

Introduction

The Agnostic's Prayer

Dear God, if there is a God;

please save my soul, if I have a soul.

Amen.

The Agnostic's Prayer probably represents the true thinking of so many people who are confused and unsure as to what or whom to believe regarding one of the most important and often thought about issues in their lives.

Throughout the history of humankind, scholars, scientists, religious leaders, theologians, and most intelligent people have pondered, researched, debated, and speculated over such issues as: *Does God really exist; is there really such a thing as a soul; and when our inevitable physical death occurs, do we permanently and completely cease to exist, or will some special part of us continue to live on; and, if so, where, how, when, in what form, and why?*

Many religions, especially those from most Christian and Jewish perspectives, express the belief that the very essence of human life, often referred to as the soul, never dies; and those souls which qualify as being worthy will spend a happy and eternal next life at some future point after their mortal lives end in a wonderful place called Heaven with a loving and all perfect Supreme Being whom they call God. Aristotle and many other leading ancient philosophers described the human psyche and the soul as being one in the same.

Some of these religions are also of the belief that the souls of the completely heinous, evil, and unforgiveable sinners who are deemed by God as unworthy of entering into an eternal happy next life in His Heaven will spend an eternity of intense and painful suffering as punishment for their Earthly sins in a miserable place called *Hell*, which has been described as a "lake of fire," and is ruled by an evil being called Satan/Lucifer/the Devil.

There are also some major Christian religions, such as Roman Catholicism, who believe there are some souls who may be considered by God to be close, but not quite yet fully worthy of or prepared to enter into the new and perfect eternal life in Heaven until they have earned His forgiveness for certain sins they may have committed by omission and/or commission while in their Earthly lives. According to this belief, these almost but not quite fully qualified souls will be required to spend a period of something akin to penance and rehabilitation time in a half-way place called *Purgatory* in order to become purged of their past Earthly sins before they will be allowed to enter into Heaven.

There are so many other varied beliefs, and they range from the ridiculous to the sublime, with some even believing that our souls are reincarnated into another form of life on Earth (e.g., your pet kitten might contain the soul of your deceased mother-in-law, a tree in the forest might contain the soul of your deceased grandfather, etc.).

There are also many who subscribe to the simple belief that when the sacks of skin filled with biochemicals, bones, organs, muscles, and flesh which constitute our Earthly bodies cease to function, we die, our bodies rot away in the ground, turn to dust, and we then completely cease to exist in any form. Many science-oriented intellectuals reject the concept of Creationism, regarding it as a self-serving manmade fantasy that is inconsistent with the laws of nature and physics; however, most will concede that it's only their "*scientific opinion*," and that they cannot produce any more absolute proof to support their non-beliefs than can most believers for their beliefs.

What do we really know, versus that which we choose to believe and can only hope to be true? For example, in the *Apostle's Creed*, which is a standard element of many Christian faith worship services, its followers begin this statement of their faith's core convictions with the words, *I believe*—but not *I know*—and the Creed then goes on to express several major statements about what was, what is, and what will be. Most major beliefs are based on reports of events that allegedly occurred thousands of years ago and are described in many often difficult to fully comprehend ancient and frequently re-translated documents such as the Holy Bible with its Old and New Testaments; Islam's Holy Quran, and numerous other ancient religion related documents whose validity and origins have been challenged by many, and for which there are many conflicting interpretations.

There are also the occasional reports of individuals who have been pronounced physically dead, and then allegedly returned to life with some incredible experiences to report…if they are, in fact, genuine, and aren't the result of a brain shut-down, an hallucinatory or delusional experience, an attention-seeking fabrication by the reporters, or a previously incorrect diagnosis of death.

Mortal life is very precious to most people, and its ending is something about which many often ponder, especially as we grow older or experience the loss of loved ones through death.

Many people go to great lengths in an effort to prolong their mortal lives; not necessarily because they are enjoying them, but only to delay the feared and mysterious experience of death. Many unhappy, depressed, or very old people's views of death are as expressed in the lyrics of the song, *Old Man River*, from the famous old Broadway hit musical, *Showboat*,: "Ah'm tired of livin' an' skeered of dyin'."

Yet, no matter how many "magic pills" or how much "snake oil" we consume that claim to extend mortal life; no matter how healthy our lifestyle; no matter how physically fit and carefully we live; no matter how many facelifts or other cosmetic surgical procedures we undergo in order to make ourselves look younger, and no matter what our genetic lifespan probabilities may be, death remains an inescapable event which we all shall experience; and most most do not know for certain when, where, how, or what, if anything, will follow. In the writing of this book, many significant pieces to the puzzle of life have finally fitted together in my mind, and have caused me to feel the most confident… not just as an acting and talking, but as a fully committed and believing Christian who shall do my best to walk the talk for however many years I have remaining in this life, and hope to be forgiven of the many sins I have committed in my present wonderful life in order to be allowed into the eternal one.

A key awareness that this deeper exploration and evaluation of the many and often directly conflicting perceptions on this major issue has produced for me is that Christianity isn't just a nice and happy sounding, history-based belief with some parts that rely heavily on faith and may be vulnerable to scientific challenge; but, more importantly, its core tenets provide its followers with *a beautiful and richly rewarding way in which to live their present lives and qualify for the one which follows.*

The book stores, internet, and library bookshelves are filled with stories that have been written about the best way to live one's life and about a life beyond this one; and this is yet another one which I hope you will find to be interesting and helpful in your own thinking about this very important matter.

Some of the names, situations, and places in the story have been fictionalized in order to honor the involved individuals' privacy, not violate confidentiality, avoid being sued, and make it more understandable and interesting reading; however, the essence of most of the characters and situations which are portrayed herein are *factual*. It is based on many readings relating to a life after this one, several in-depth interviews with individuals who have reported having experienced physical death and returned to mortal life with some very interesting, believable, and encouraging stories to report.

My readings on this topic have included the Holy Bible from Genesis through Revelations, Dr. George Ritchie's excellent autobiographical book, *Ordered to Return…My Life After Dying; Don Piper's 90 Minutes in Heaven; Dr. Elisabeth Kubler-Ross's series of books beginning with On Death and Dying; Billy Graham's The Heaven Answer Book; Steve Sjogren's, The Day I Died; Dr. Mary Neal's To Heaven and Back; Judy Bachrach's Glimpsing Heaven, Charles Colson's Loving God,* and several others. These well-researched, well-written, and highly credible books that have been written by sound-minded and well-informed people, along with my personal experiences and those of others which they have shared with me, have combined to cause me to comfortably conclude that the soul and a beautiful life beyond this one are real!

Ed Vaughn

Chapter One

On a warm, clear, and beautiful early September evening, Timothy Dickson McDonald, called "Tim" by his friends and family, sat alone on the railing of the upstairs rear balcony in the backyard of his rural Dumont, North Carolina home, located in Cumberland County, and a few miles from the larger city of Fayetteville. As he slowly sipped on a glass of cabernet sauvignon wine, Tim viewed the beautiful setting sun and listened to the gentle ringing chimes of a nearby church, the sound of chirping crickets, and the soft fluttering sounds of several humming birds that were partaking of a liquid feeder located near him on the balcony. This tranquil setting was providing a much needed calming effect on Tim's heavily loaded psyche.

He didn't want to break the effect of this serene setting by looking through the sliding glass doors behind him and observing the many packed boxes that were stacked up inside his home, as what they represented would interfere with the rare peaceful and tranquil state of mind he was enjoying. His wife and sister had taken complete charge of the packing process and made it quite clear to him that it was their project and they didn't want him in their way, which was just fine with Tim!

Most of the furniture that Tim and his family had enjoyed having in their home for the past few years had been left under the car port earlier in the day to be picked up in the morning by buyers from Craig's List and others from their earlier huge yard sale. Those few larger things that were especially sentimental remembrances of their soon to be past lives in Cumberland County that they couldn't take with them to their future home would be stored elsewhere for an indefinite period.

Tim felt a slight touch of sadness as he thought of the farewell dinner that he and his family had shared with his aging parents at their home on the previous evening, which could possibly be their last time together in this life, and the bon voyage party that some of their friends at the hospital had held for them on the evening before. Both of these events were celebrating the final chapter of a major part of

Tim's old life and the beginning of a new and highly challenging one for him and his family. After the many past changes that had occurred in his life and yet another major change was about to occur, Tim welcomed this rare, albeit brief, break from the several recent turbulent stressors he had experienced, and was enjoying this peaceful setting. He then began to reminisce over the many significant and incredible life-shaping events he had thus far experienced in his journey on the road of life.

* * * * * *

Tim's first thoughts were of the many blessings he had enjoyed in his earlier life, especially his wonderful birth family, consisting of his father, John; his mother, Ruth, and his three years younger sister, Amelia, and he reflected on his experiences with each of them and the important roles they had thus far played in the shaping of his life.

He had been raised by his parents in their comfortable and luxurious four thousand square foot brick home that was beautifully landscaped, had a large in ground swimming pool, and was located on a large lakefront lot in the upscale Cedar Lakes section of the small, unincorporated Cumberland County town of Dumont, North Carolina. Cumberland County had been Tim's family's ancestral home for at least six generations since his paternal ancestors sailed to America from Skye, Scotland in the seventeenth century.

Tim's father was an exceptionally bright, strikingly handsome, very successful, and well respected trial attorney and senior partner in an old, large, and highly regarded law firm in the nearby city of Fayetteville. He had always been a loving and devoted father to Tim and his younger sister; a deeply committed, loving and faithful husband to their mother; a long-term active member and office holder in several important community service organizations such as the Lions, Kiwanis, and Rotary Clubs; a frequent volunteer at the Salvation Army and Fayetteville Urban Ministry, and a member of the vestry (lay persons' leadership group) of the beautiful and historic old St. Thomas Episcopal Church in the charming little town of Dumont, where several generations of his family had been active members since its beginning back in the middle eighteenth century. In short, Tim's father was a world-class pillar of the community and a great role model for his children.

His father was born and raised in Fayetteville by his successful and well-respected parents. Tim's deceased grandfather, Alton, who was a retired US Army Colonel, had received his bachelor's degree in civil engineering at the United States Military Academy at West Point and master's degree from the University of South Carolina; his deceased grandmother, Elizabeth, held a Master's degree in Education from North Carolina State University and had been a high school English teacher in Fayetteville; his uncle, Eric, was a medical doctor in the nearby town of Hamlet; and his younger cousin, Warren, a Ph.D. and Department Chairperson at the Methodist University in Fayetteville. Education and achievement had always been very high priorities in the McDonald family.

After Tim's father had earned his Bachelor of Science degree in Business Administration from the then Methodist College (now University), where he completed the Army ROTC program, he received a commission in the United States Army as an Infantry Second Lieutenant, and was immediately ordered to active duty.

He completed the Basic Infantry Officer's Course, Ranger and Airborne training at Fort Benning, Georgia, and then served as an infantry platoon leader with the 101st Airborne Division during the war in the former Republic of South Viet Nam. This was the same military unit in which John's father had served long before him, and had later retired from the Army as an Infantry Colonel.

While serving in combat during the historic 1968 Tet Offensive by the North Vietnamese Army in the Ashau Valley region of South Viet Nam, Tim's father was badly wounded in his shoulder when he courageously moved through intense enemy fire to save the life of one of his wounded soldiers, and was awarded the Silver Star and Purple Heart medals for his gallantry and wounds.

Due to the severity of his combat wounds, he was later medically discharged from the Army as a Captain. Then, with the financial aid that was provided to him by the G.I. Bill of Rights, he earned his law degree from the University Of North Carolina School Of Law, and soon became one of the leading trial attorneys in Cumberland County.

* * * * * *

Tim's mother, the former Ruth Dickson, was born in Fayetteville and raised by her widowed, uneducated, disabled, alcohol and drug addicted mother in a rundown trailer park that was located in one of the poorest sections of town.

Ruth had no recollection of her father, who worked on the old Seaboard Coast Line Railroad as a fireman and had been killed in a railroad train accident when Ruth was an infant. Her pathetic mother then had multiple subsequent male relationships, all of short duration, and died of a drug overdose when Ruth was sixteen years old and beginning her senior year of high school. Ruth had no other known living blood relatives except an uncle, her mother's older brother, who was serving a lengthy sentence in a Federal Prison after his third conviction for the manufacturing and selling of methamphetamines and other illegal drugs.

Despite her highly deprived and turbulent childhood and having been left alone in the world to fend for herself at a very young age, Ruth was strongly determined to do all she could to rise above her early life's miserable circumstances.

With the support of a large academic scholarship she had earned while in high school, and by working as an office cleaning person on weekday nights and as a waitress at the Waffle House restaurant on weekend nights, she was able to earn her Bachelor of Science degree in Nursing from the Fayetteville State University, where she graduated at the top of her class.

She was a hard striving, clean living, and very intelligent young lady who served as the youngest ever deaconess at the First Christian Church in Fayetteville, where she also sang in the church's choir and taught a children's Sunday school class.

Ruth was a very attractive, high achieving, and all-around accomplished young woman who had also been a soprano soloist in the University's and her church's choir, and had won the Miss Cumberland County beauty contest.

After her graduation, she passed the State Nursing Board examination with the highest score ever recorded at that time, and then began her professional career as a registered nurse, where she served in an operating room at the Cumberland County Regional Medical Center that was located between Dumont and Fayetteville.

She was also commissioned as an officer in the U.S. Army Reserve Nurses Corps and performed her monthly weekend reserve duties at the nearby Fort Bragg, North Carolina, Womack Army Medical Center.

* * * * * *

Tim's Mom loved to tell the story of how she and Tim's father first met one Saturday morning when he was a patient at the Womack Army Medical Center where he was receiving rehabilitation treatment for the wounds he had suffered while serving in South Viet Nam, and she was performing her monthly weekend duty as a First Lieutenant in the Army Reserve Nurses Corps.

Early in the morning, as Ruth was entering the hospital's front door, she slipped on the freshly waxed floor and John, who was standing close by, reached out and caught her just before she fell. As he held her in his arms, they found themselves briefly staring into each other's eyes and Ruth quickly intuitively sensed that this was no simple accident, but a possibly Divinely-caused beginning of a very special relationship.

It was indeed love at first sight for both of them, and John proposed to Ruth within two months after their accidental meeting. They were later married in the St. Thomas Episcopal Church in Dumont while he was attending law school, and were soon the parents of two children, a son, Timothy, and a three years younger daughter, Amelia.

Ruth became a devoted mother and wife who also served as a regular volunteer at the Fayetteville CARE Clinic, the Salvation Army, and several other local charities; an active member of the Dumont Women's Club; President of her children's school PTA; a lay reader in John's family's church, St. Thomas Episcopal Church, and a leading soprano in the church's magnificent choir. Like her husband, Ruth was also an exemplary citizen and role model for their two children.

* * * * * *

One of the earliest major memorable events of Tim's early childhood, which he clearly recalled as though it happened only yesterday, was one that occurred one evening when he was six-years-old and in the first grade.

As he did every night during his early childhood, Tim knelt beside his bed, attired in his cotton flannel "trap-door" pajamas with his hands clasped together, his head reverently bowed, and his loving mother kneeling alongside him, and said his regular nightly prayer:

Now I lay me down to sleep, and I pray the Lord my soul to keep. If I should die before I wake, I pray the Lord my soul to take. Amen.

This was a nightly routine in which Tim and his little sister had participated since they were old enough to recite the words of the long time popular children's bedtime prayer.

After Tim had finished saying his nightly prayer, he arose from his knees and jumped into his bed. His loving mother then gently tucked him in, tickled and shared giggles with him, and then gave him a warm hug and a soft goodnight kiss on his forehead as she had done every night.

He clearly recalled one particular night when, after saying his bedtime prayer, he had asked his mother if she would stay with him for a few minutes before she turned out the light and explain some things that were weighing heavily on his mind.

She sweetly replied, "Sure, Honey, but please make it real quick because it's time for you to go nighty-night since you have to get up early in the morning to get ready for school. What is it that you want to talk about with me?"

Tim told her that he wanted to know who the Lord was and where He lived. He said he was referring to this person that he had never seen before and called Lord when he would say his bedtime prayers every night, and asked to take his soul if he should die before he woke up.

His mother replied, "Why, son, He is the Father of all of us; the wonderful one who created us and the whole universe; the one who takes care of us every day of our lives, and the one who will always love and guide us in the right direction. He lives with His beloved Son, our precious Savior, Jesus Christ, and His many angels in a beautiful place called Heaven."

Tim then asked her what this place called Heaven was like, and if it was close enough that they might be able to go there and see it sometime, and asked why Jesus didn't have a sister, too.

She said, "No, Honey; Heaven is a beautiful and happy place that's way up in the sky and far, far away from this world, and people only get to go there when their lives on Earth are over. And, no, Jesus didn't have a sister but I can't tell you why."

He then asked what his soul was, the thing that he would always say in his prayer that he wants the Lord to take from him when he died.

She replied, "Your soul is the most important and precious part of you, my dear son; and although you can't see it, it's deep inside you and it will live on forever and ever."

Tim asked if she meant that his soul would still be alive even after he gets real old and dies like his paternal grandmother did the year before.

She replied, "That's right, son; when our bodies finally die, our souls will leave this world; and if we've been good boys and girls and have obeyed God's laws, our souls will then go to Heaven like I'm sure your dear Grandma's did, and they will happily live there forever with our Lord God and His beloved Son, Jesus Christ."

Tim then asked what would happen to his soul if he wasn't a good boy; like if he had been a really, really bad boy and didn't always obey God's laws.

At this point, his mother was becoming impatient over the seemingly endless barrage of questions that Tim was asking and seemed to really want answers for.

She rolled her eyes upward and replied with a sigh, "Well, son, some really bad people might go to an awful place that's called Hell, but we don't need to talk about that right now since it's never going to happen to you anyhow, because I know you will always be my good boy."

She finally brought their talk to an end by raising her hands and firmly saying, "Now please stop asking me so many questions, Timmy. You must get to sleep because it's getting real late and you've got to get up early for school tomorrow." She then turned off his bedroom light, left the room, and closed the door.

* * * * * *

But as hard as he tried, Tim was unable to fall asleep right away. Instead, he lay awake for a long while, tossing and turning as he pondered the answers his mother had given him; but they just didn't sufficiently answer his questions, nor did they seem to make much sense to Tim. To him, they were basically nothing more than a lot of too brief and very confusing esoteric words and concepts that he wasn't able to fully comprehend.

After Tim had closed his eyes and was trying to fall asleep, the conversation he had just shared with his mother continued to generate even more troubling questions that kept swirling through his young mind for a good part of the evening.

He thought to himself, *Why did Mommy not want to tell me more about what that bad place called Hell is about; where did this Lord God who made me come from and who made Him; who is Jesus and why does God have just a son and not a daughter; what does a soul really look like, and where is this beautiful place called Heaven really located? There's just no way that it can be way up in the sky like Mommy told me, or it would fall down to the ground and crash. How can God and Jesus hear me and everybody else in the world saying all their prayers to them at once, and how can they see me and know whether or not I've been a good boy and obeyed some laws all the time if they are really in a place that's so far away up in the sky?*

These and many other confusing questions continued to swirl through Tim's young mind and he was having a very difficult time in trying to fall asleep.

When he awakened early the next morning, Tim's mind was still troubled over his thoughts from the night before and he was determined that he had to somehow find some better and more understandable answers to these troubling questions than the brief and hard to comprehend ones his mother had provided.

During the next day, the questions about the words in his nighttime prayer just wouldn't go out of his young mind. He was disciplined by his school teacher for not paying attention in class; the following day he forgot to take his lunch to school, and then forgot to take his baseball glove to his Little League baseball team's practice on Saturday…all of which were due to his continuing mental preoccupation over the same issues that had kept him awake for half of the night earlier in the week.

The next Sunday morning, Tim, his father, mother, and little sister, Amelia, went to church together as they always had. Unlike most children of his young age who were often restless and inattentive during the adult worship service, Tim listened intently to every word spoken by the priest, the Reverend Allen Roberts, in his sermon and prayers, especially when he made frequent references to God, Heaven, Jesus, praying, and the soul.

But instead of shedding more light on the issues that had become so confusing and troubling to Tim, the things the priest said in his sermon and prayers only generated more questions into his young mind than they provided understandable answers for, and this added more fuel to the fire of his continuing confused and growing curiosity. To Tim, it was just more of what he began to think of as "God talk," and most of it didn't make a bit of sense to him.

After the church service was over, Tim and his family returned to their home and sat down at the dining room table to have their lunch. As they always did prior to unfolding their napkins, they held their hands together and bowed their heads while his father said the blessing, where he was supposedly talking directly with God, and his father's words only served to continue triggering even more questions into Tim's young mind... more confusing "God talk!"

Tim's curiosity over all of this talk about God, Jesus, Heaven, praying, and the soul continued to be a troubling obsession with him for several days and he had an intense desire to understand what it was all about.

However, after a few days of unsuccessfully trying to make understandable sense out of these things that were confusing and troubling to him, Tim's sudden surge of interest in spiritual and religious matters began to fade and he was finally able to put them out of his mind.

It wasn't that Tim didn't still want some understandable answers to his questions, because he desperately did; but he finally concluded that they were just either not forthcoming or were too far beyond his young level of understanding. He decided that he had to cease in his frustrating thinking about them and just accept that what he was being told was true and stop worrying about it.

Instead of allowing himself to worry any longer about these questions for which there seemed to be no answers that made sense to him, Tim shifted his full attention back to the things which were important to him during that period of his life and which he had a better understanding and control of, such as his schoolwork, friends, family, and little league baseball. The previous sudden infusion of curiosity about spiritual matters then gradually began to fade away from his young mind and no longer concerned him.

Chapter Two

During the summer prior to when Tim's very bright, cute and loveable little sister, Amelia, was scheduled to begin the first grade of school, a terrible tragedy occurred when she fell from a pony at the church's summer camp for children and suffered a severe injury to her spinal cord. The injury nearly ended her life, and initially caused her little body to be completely paralyzed from the neck down.

Tim, along with his parents, spent many anxious days in the hospital at Amelia's bedside, as she was barely alive and the likelihood of her surviving her injuries seemed remote.

Fortunately, Amelia did survive after undergoing several intensive and complex surgical procedures to repair her injuries were performed by a Doctor Bruce Jaufman, reputed to be the best neurosurgeon in the area, and most of the neurological functioning above her waistline was finally restored.

However, it was finally concluded by her doctor that nothing further could be done for little Amelia, and it was highly unlikely that her condition would ever improve beyond where it was. Dr. Jaufman sadly advised her parents that he had done all that could be done for her without putting her life at greater risk, and Amelia would probably remain paralyzed from the waist down and not be able to walk for the remainder of her life.

This very bright and beautiful, but severely handicapped little child then became dependent on a wheelchair in order to get around, and had to be transported by her parents along with her wheelchair strapped to their car nearly everywhere she went.

A few months later, Amelia suffered an additional debilitating injury when the school bus driver foolishly attempted to load her wheelchair onto the bus with her sitting in it. She fell from it and onto the road, striking her head on the hard pavement.

This mishap resulted in severe damage occurring to her optic nerves and caused her to become nearly totally blind. A nearby leading ophthalmological surgeon, Dr. Wayne Riggins, worked diligently to restore her eyesight and was able to restore much of it; but he sadly advised her parents that he had done everything possible to help her and, in order for her to be able to see, Amelia would have to wear corrective lens that were nearly a quarter of an inch thick for the remainder of her life.

But dear little Amelia didn't allow these unfortunate physical setbacks in her young life to hold her down! Although she was unable to enjoy the pleasure of playing games and running outdoors with other children, she directed her mental energy into becoming a prolific reader and was reading on a high school level and had become highly competent in her creative clay sculpturing hobby by the time she was only ten years old.

At the age of eleven, Amelia had a showing of her clay sculptures at the Fayetteville Arts Council Building, from which she received rave reviews by art critics from around the state. She was an extremely intelligent, attractive, talented, well-liked, and well-behaved little girl who always made straight A's in school in spite of her severe physical handicaps.

With her very talented mother's help, Amelia also developed a beautiful singing voice and, at the age of twelve, she became the youngest ever member of the St. Thomas Episcopal Church's highly regarded choir where she sang a lovely solo of *Amazing Grace* one Sunday that was lauded by the congregation.

Amelia was described by Bill Kirby, a local, widely read, and highly respected newspaper writer in his regular *Fayetteville Observer* column as "A budding little Super Star who has set an inspiring example by her positive attitude and achievements, not only for other handicapped children, but for *all of us to follow*."

Bill Bowman, the publisher of a popular local weekly publication in Fayetteville, *Up and Coming Magazine*, wrote a full-page lengthy pictorial editorial about Amelia's many talents and achievements, and this added to her becoming quite a little celebrity in Cumberland County!

Tim was very proud of and adored his little sister, always tried to be there to protect her, and would give her any assistance she asked of him.

* * * * * *

Tim's paternal grandfather, Alton, an elderly retired US Army Colonel whom Tim called "Pop," and Tim had been each other's very best buddies since Tim was about five years old. On many weekends and during his summer vacations, Pop would take Tim fishing with him out into the Atlantic Ocean on the twenty-eight foot Stamas fishing boat that he kept docked at Carolina Beach.

Pop also taught Tim to play golf at the Highland Country Club, the beautiful Fayetteville golf course and country club where Pop was one of the leading golfers in the seventy-five years of age and older senior men's golf group. Tim had always held Pop on a high pedestal as his biggest hero and very best friend in his life!

Shortly after Tim's thirteenth birthday, his grandfather, who had been a two pack a day cigarette smoker for the majority of his life, passed away due to lung cancer at the age of eighty-nine. Prior to his funeral and burial, Tim, his parents, and sister attended the final viewing of Pop's body at a local funeral home.

As Tim sadly observed his deceased grandfather's body lying cold and still in the casket, and looking more like a lifeless wax mannequin than the very active and fun loving best friend that he had known him as being all of his life, Tim tearfully reminisced over the many happy times they had shared while playing golf and going fishing together, and knew he would sorely miss him.

The same issues regarding spiritual matters that had been troubling to Tim seven years earlier suddenly came flowing back into his mind when he heard his Dad comment to his Mom that his beloved grandfather's soul was now enjoying an eternal and happy life in Heaven with our

God and His Son, Jesus Christ…more "God talk" again!

Tim then again made up his mind that he had to know more of what God, Jesus, Heaven, the soul, and death were all about, so he resumed his determined quest to find acceptable answers to these issues that had troubled him earlier in his life.

Tim had always been an avid reader and began spending many hours in the church and school libraries scanning through as many books as he could find that dealt with God, Jesus, the soul, Heaven, and reports of people who had returned to life after experiencing death, in search of some more logical and believable answers to the questions that had again begun to confuse and trouble him.

But it seemed that the more Tim researched these topics, the more frustrated he became from what he perceived as many conflicting and seemingly weak and poorly supported theories that his research was producing, and the majority of the theories were based on quotes from the Holy Bible, whose validity he had also begun to seriously question.

After several days of intensive research about Christianity and many other varying religious beliefs, Tim finally concluded that the many different theories he had read and heard about from others on the subject were no more than that, theories…peoples' guesses and hopes that were primarily based upon ancient documents, with various and often major conflicting interpretations of them, along with questionable reports from several people who had allegedly returned back to mortal life after having been declared physically dead.

To Tim, there just weren't enough convincing, indisputable, or scientifically provable hard facts to satisfy his serious inquiry…just a lot of more confusing "God talk" that raised more questions in his mind than they answered.

For several weeks, in his troubled mind Tim had almost constantly pondered over such questions as: *How could the trillions of people who had died over thousands of years possibly reside in this place called Heaven and be without any individual physical form; how could God or Jesus know how good or bad these trillions of individuals had been for every moment in their lives; how could God hear and respond to the billions of prayers that were being said by people every day; who were God and Jesus and where did they come from; how could anything or anyone have neither a beginning nor an end to them, and why do Christians wear a cross to signify their belief in Jesus since being nailed to it was what caused him to die? If this so-called Son of God had been stabbed, stoned, or hung instead of dying on a cross, would Christians be wearing a knife, rock, or a rope around their necks instead of a cross?*

Very little of what Tim had heard from others and read about in books meshed well with his reasoning. To him, much of it was still nothing but a lot of unsupported and difficult to understand and believe religious babble - what he now frequently and sarcastically referred to others as "God talk!"

Out of his troubling mental frustration over these issues, Tim eventually concluded that he had to stop worrying himself sick about something that made no sense at all to him and to which no one appeared to really know the answers; so he once again gave up in his confusing and unsuccessful quest for some more acceptable answers.

He even completely ceased saying his prayers, as it only frustrated him to do so since it made no sense at all to him that God, Jesus, or any single being, could possibly be able to listen and respond to him and hundreds of millions of other people communicating with them all at once. Praying just seemed to be a complete waste of Tim's time when his logic told him that no one could possibly be listening to his prayers, and praying had only served to trigger even more frustrating and troubling questions into his young mind.

* * * * * *

Shortly after he reached the age of fifteen, Tim shared his spiritual and intellectually frustrating dilemma with Jerry "Red" Hart, an older, tall, and red-haired high school classmate and close friend with whom Tim frequently hung out, played with on their high school's football, basketball, and baseball teams, and in whose judgment Tim held a high respect.

Red told Tim that he had also gone through the same frustrating experience in trying to understand the crazy stuff about religion in his life as Tim was having in his. He said that he had finally given up in trying to make any logical sense out of his family's Roman Catholic religion, and had made the decision to embrace Atheism instead because it wasn't as confusing and was a much simpler and logical way of dealing with the issue.

Red also told Tim that he had found accepting Atheism to be a more believable, and less troubling approach to take than trying to make sense out of things which were so complicated, seemingly illogical, fraught with contradictions, and were often deeply annoying as most of his family's religious beliefs had become to him.

Although Red's liberal parents were active members of a local Roman Catholic Church, out of frustration over his frequent and annoying challenges of their religious beliefs, they had chosen to allow him to follow his own beliefs rather than forcing theirs upon him because he had embarrassed them too many times in his disbelieving and somewhat rudely outspoken confrontations with their priest and friends, and had developed some negative attitudes toward his church and its teachings that were very similar to Tim's.

After having several lengthy discussions about the subject of religion with Red, Tim became convinced that he should also consider ceasing his frustrating struggle to understand and accept Christianity and become an Atheist which, to him, was simpler and made more practical sense.

Red invited Tim to join a small and clandestine group of student Atheists at their high school. It was clandestine because the prevailing attitude at Cumberland County High School was that everyone in their school was expected to be a believer in God and would be ostracized if they weren't, so they had to stay undercover with their new Atheism.

Tim accepted his friend's invitation and then officially became a proud Atheist, and he was relieved to cease worrying about those things that had previously bothered him so much since his earlier childhood. There would be no more struggling with "God talk" for Tim, the newly committed Atheist! Tim's parents were becoming concerned about the defiant and outspokenly negative attitude that Tim had developed towards religion since choosing to become an Atheist, and he had begun to express strong criticism towards the church and their family's religious beliefs; and no matter what form of reasoning they used in their attempts to dissuade him from his Atheism and cause him to return back into Christianity, nothing seemed to change his increasingly hardened views.

After failing in their many frustrating attempts to convince Tim that his way of thinking was erroneous, his parents discussed their concerns about him with a clinical psychologist who was also a member of their church.

At his parents' request, the psychologist met with Tim and, unbeknownst to them, Tim saw a copy of the psychologist's written assessment which had been given to Tim's parents. It concluded that Tim, being what the psychologist perceived to be an otherwise highly intelligent young man, was simply going through a brief and not unusual sophomoric and defiant developmental stage in his spiritual, social, and intellectual processing with his newly professed atheistic beliefs, a stage that was not uncommon among children in the middle to late adolescence phase that Tim was in.

The psychologist's report also suggested to Tim's parents that if they would give him enough time, were patient with him, and didn't insist that he participate in their religious activities for a little while, he would probably eventually grow out of his atheism, see the light, and then return to the church to re-embrace the family's strong religious beliefs.

Otherwise, Tim had always tried to be a nice young man by being polite, well-mannered and behaved, except where religion was concerned, and his angry rejection towards it showed; was kind to and gladly helping to his badly handicapped little sister; maintained the family's beautiful lawn; was respectful and obedient to his parents; made excellent grades in school, and was a pretty good player on his high school's football, basketball, and baseball teams. Tim aspired to go to college after finishing high school and someday become a medical doctor.

Chapter Three

Tim had a steady girlfriend by the name of Sarah Townsend whom he first met when they were in the seventh grade together and her family lived a few houses down on the same street in the upscale little town of Dumont as Tim's.

Sarah and Tim later attended Cumberland County High School together. She was an exceptionally attractive and bright young girl with curly blonde hair and sparkling blue-eyes who had placed second in the North Carolina State's Miss Teenage America competition; a solid A+ student who was in several of Tim's classes; played on the girls' softball and soccer teams; was the lead high school football cheerleader; helped to maintain her family's beautiful lawn; was an excellent pianist; sang in the high school's chorus, and was of the very highest moral character.

She also regularly attended St. Thomas Episcopal Church with her parents where she often assisted in the infants' nursery, served as an acolyte during many Sunday worship services, taught a Vacation Bible School class for pre-school and handicapped children, and enjoyed a perfect church and school attendance record. Sarah was an absolutely perfect teenage girl in every way!

She would often visit Amelia at the McDonald home and assist Tim with his little sister when he would take her out in her wheelchair for a stroll around the neighborhood on good weather days. Sarah's growing fondness for Amelia and the kind help she would give her further served to bond Sarah and Tim together as each other's very best friend.

Tim's often strongly outspoken criticism of religion and the church was the only significant issue of disagreement between him and Sarah; but, just as his parents had done, she also chose to patiently view Tim's claim of being an Atheist as part of a transitory developmental process that was associated with his very high intellect and youthful age, and also assumed that he would eventually see the light and grow out of it. Otherwise, Sarah adored Tim and his family, and they adored her.

Like Tim, Sarah also aspired to a future in medicine.

* * * * * *

At their high school graduation ceremony, where Sarah was selected to serve as the class valedictorian, both she and Tim received special recognition and several honors for their many athletic and academic achievements.

But, to their parents' and Sarah's chagrin, Tim expressed his very strong anti-religion feelings when he outwardly and intentionally non-verbally showed his disapproving attitude by standing and defiantly turning his head away from the podium, crossing his arms, shaking his head from side to side, and angrily frowning his disapproval when a local Roman Catholic priest and a Jewish rabbi gave the invocation and benediction for the graduation ceremony.

He embarrassed and offended nearly everyone present, especially Sarah and their parents, with this hostile and inappropriate gesture, but they had no choice but to let it pass as they had with Tim's other often offensive expressions of his new Atheistic beliefs.

Sarah and Tim had chosen to attend the top-notch Methodist University in nearby Fayetteville together in a pre-med program, where they both majored in biology. As it had been for them during their high school days, while undergraduate students at Methodist University they were nearly inseparable.

They took most of the same classes together where they always sat next to one another, had the same sets of friends, studied together, shared nearly every lunch time together, and rode to and from the University together every day.

Sarah would also often sit in the bleachers at the baseball field and cheer for Tim when he had baseball practice and played in their University's games. She even made certain that she wouldn't have a class scheduled at the same time as Tim's Army ROTC drill sessions, so she could enjoy proudly watching him as he marched on the parade field in his snazzy Army uniform.

The two of them did pretty much everything together…except go inside a church, which Tim had now absolutely refused to do for any reason; not even to attend the funeral of one of his close friends who had been killed in an automobile accident. Tim just didn't want anything to do with the church or religion, period!

Over the years that followed, instead of changing his Atheistic views and returning to his family's traditional Christian religious beliefs as his parents and Sarah had hoped and the psychologist had predicted that he might eventually do, his commitment to Atheism and rejection of Christianity only continued to grow even deeper and more uncompromising as he grew older.

He not only rejected his family's and Sarah's traditional Christian beliefs as being illogical and foolish fantasies, he openly and angrily scorned them and especially the church, which he believed and criticized as being an evil and fraudulent scam of an organization that was dedicated to the propagation of fabricated historical stories for the main purpose of controlling their constituents' minds and money. While in college, he remained in frequent contact with his old pal, Red, and the other Atheist Club members from his high school days.

Tim and Sarah eventually earned their Bachelor of Science degrees in biology from Methodist University, with both graduating summa cum laude, and they were accepted as students at the University of North Carolina's School of Medicine. Tim was also commissioned as a Second Lieutenant in the US Army Reserves and attended the three-month Basic Infantry Officer's Course at Fort Benning, Georgia just prior to their beginning medical school.

Afterwards, Tim would have to spend a weekend of Army Reserve training at an armory in Fayetteville once each month and two weeks away for training during the summer, which Sarah always dreaded because they would miss each other terribly; however, she was very proud of him for serving and they would exchange frequent telephone calls while he was away.

* * * * * *

They then began their studies at the University of North Carolina Medical School in Chapel Hill that fall where Tim and Sarah continued to remain nearly inseparable…except on Sunday mornings when Sarah would attend worship services at the University's Chapel, always by herself and never with Tim, the now firmly committed and very outspoken Atheist.

As a key part of their medical education, Tim and Sarah often worked with human cadavers in the medical school laboratory to study the anatomical structures and functions of the human body.

In Tim's atheistic mind, the cadavers were nothing more than the dead remains of people whose lives had permanently ended and he viewed them with no particular feelings, but only as lifeless flesh, biochemicals, organs, muscles, and bones to be studied; however, Sarah viewed them quite differently.

She viewed the cadavers as the Earthly remains of people whose essence, their souls, had been separated from them upon their physical death and who were now living happily with God in Heaven for all of eternity—and she treated them with a special respect by often saying a quiet prayer in honor of their departed souls prior to engaging in her study of them.

Tim would occasionally walk in on Sarah in the laboratory while she was saying a prayer for their souls and she would vainly attempt to explain her view of the soul to Tim.

But Tim would usually respond to her explanation with a condescending grin, shake his head in annoyed disbelief, and say such sarcastic things as "You can believe whatever the heck you want to, Sarah, but you should keep your stupid religious fantasies to yourself because I happen to know better…and so will you someday when you wise up and grow out of believing all that phony, fairy tale religious bull crap that we have been force-fed by that evil and self-serving church for most of our lives."

Hearing such often caustic and sarcastic comments from Tim that were critical of her spiritual beliefs would cause Sarah to cringe and grit her teeth in angry frustration, but she wouldn't dare say anything in response to his scathing remarks. She knew it would only be a waste of her breath to do so, and would usually generate more angry and sarcastic ranting from him. But she still otherwise adored the good that she saw in Tim, despite the enormously polarized differences in their beliefs about spiritual and religious matters.

They both graduated from the UNC School of Medicine with highest honors, and were accepted to serve their medical internships at the Cumberland County Regional Medical Center that was conveniently located between Fayetteville and their home town of Dumont.

* * * * * *

After Tim and Sarah had graduated from the University Of North Carolina School Of Medicine and Tim had finished his two weeks of annual Army Reserve summer training at Fort Jackson, South Carolina, both were back home in Dumont and scheduled to begin their medical internships in the coming month.

Tim invited Sarah to join him for dinner one evening, and they drove over to Fayetteville where they enjoyed a very romantic dinner together at their favorite restaurant, the classic old Hilltop House, located in the historic Haymont section of Fayetteville.

After they had finished dinner, Tim got down on a bended knee before Sarah and asked her to marry him. He offered her a three-karat diamond engagement ring that was set in platinum and had belonged to his deceased grandmother, and asked that their marriage take place as soon as possible since they were scheduled to begin their internships in the coming month.

Sarah happily accepted Tim's proposal and he proudly slipped the beautiful engagement ring onto her finger. They then held each other closely, kissed, and exchanged "I love yous" while the other patrons in the restaurant stood and happily applauded them.

Afterwards, they returned to Sarah's new town house condominium which her parents had given her as a graduation gift and was located a few miles closer to the hospital, where they happily sat together at her dining room table with pencils and note pads to put together the details for their forthcoming wedding.

Unfortunately, what was intended to be a happy wedding planning discussion for Tim and Sarah precipitated their first-ever really major argument.

The argument began when Tim expressed his preference that the wedding should take place outdoors in a gazebo at the nearby beautiful Fayetteville Botanical Garden with a judge, justice of the peace, magistrate, or some other authorized and non-religious person to conduct a purely secular type of marriage ceremony...anyone but an ordained religious person.

But Sarah firmly responded with her strong disagreement over his choice and was adamant that their wedding ceremony should be a traditional Christian one and must take place in St. Thomas Episcopal Church in Dumont, which both of their families and many of their friends had attended all of their lives, and it must be officiated by their friendly and highly respected priest, Reverend Allen Roberts.

The disagreement over where, who would officiate, and in what format the wedding should take place soon escalated into a heated and angry argument between them which became very hostile, grew far out of control, and was beginning to place their long-term close and loving relationship and only two-hour old engagement into serious jeopardy.

Tim became highly vituperative and began to raise his voice and bang his fist on the table as he expressed some very harsh, inflammatory, and anger-driven insults at Sarah by saying such things as "I just cannot understand how someone as intelligent and educated as you are supposed to be could be stupid enough to still believe all that fairy tale bull crap that the dumb and self-serving church has fed your naïve head with all of your life."

He also told her that if their getting married meant that he had to accept and participate in "all that phony church bull crap" for the rest of their lives, she could just forget about their getting married and give him back the engagement ring.

With that harsh comment from Tim, Sarah let her temper fly and angrily shouted back at him, "The church does not fill my head with what you call 'phony church bull crap', Mister Know-it-All! It's my choice to believe in what my church teaches and represents to me, which I definitely do and always will; but I'm beginning to believe that it's you who are a stupid jerk, dumb ass, and the phony one who is full of bull crap, and not the church. I wish you would grow up and drop your stupid and immature atheistic bull crap, Tim; because if you don't, you can just forget about our getting married, and get the hell out of my life forever as far as I'm concerned!"

From that point on, their argument further escalated into a bitter verbal war of even more rude expletives and personal insults being exchanged between them over their conflicting beliefs.

Tim finally completely emotionally exploded and jumped up from the table, kicked a hole in the dining room wall, angrily threw the tablet down on the floor, and then prepared to storm out of Sarah's home in a rage. He shouted that he never again wanted to see or speak to her or anyone who was as hard headed and stupid as she.

Sarah angrily ordered him to get out of her home and life, and never come back. She removed the engagement ring from her finger that he had given her earlier that evening and threw it at him; then angrily slammed and locked the front door of her home after Tim left. She then cried for hours and stayed deeply depressed for days!

* * * * * *

The week that followed their explosive argument was the longest period of time that Sarah and Tim had not spoken to one another in the twelve years since they first met when they were both just twelve years old.

Tim then found himself in the most unhappy and darkest period of his young life, during which time he did something he had never done before; he began to drink alcohol - lots of it - to help numb the terrible pain that existed in his hurting mind over the breakup with Sarah.

Out of angry defiance, he also started smoking cigarettes and began to hang out in some of the local raunchy strip clubs on Bragg Boulevard in Fayetteville in an attempt to erase thoughts of Sarah from his deeply depressed, lonely, and guilt-ridden state of mind. He was even once approached by a prostitute who tempted him but, fortunately, he decided against following through with her solicitation when he realized that he would be committing an unforgiveable offense against Sarah if their relationship should ever resume.

One night, while he was hanging out with Red and his other Atheist high school buddies, was very drunk and feeling nearly totally uninhibited, Tim even had a small tattoo engraved on his left shoulder with an upside-down cross, to express his rejection of Christianity.

* * * * * *

Finally, early one morning a week after having had his awful fight with Sarah and having engaged in a heavy drinking binge at a strip club bar the previous night, Tim awakened with a terrible hangover and a painful infection from the ugly tattoo on his shoulder.

He felt extremely depressed and angry towards himself for his week of foolish and inappropriate behavior, especially for his way out of character meanness towards his dear Sarah, and was generally disgusted with this new miserable and low-class choice of activities.

Tim had finally arrived at the clear conclusion that this kind of low-class lifestyle wasn't for him and, most of all, his heart was badly aching to be back with his precious Sarah. He was determined that, whatever it would take to make it happen, he was going to somehow get back with her, the sorely missed and greatest love of his life outside of his immediate family.

As he lay in his bed and pondered the situation, Tim finally made the decision that he had to make his best effort to get Sarah back into his life as quickly as possible. He jumped out of the bed, shaved and showered, dressed in his best suit, drove to a local florist and bought a dozen red roses. He then went to her home and rang the doorbell. When she opened the front door, he handed her the roses, dropped to his knees, and tearfully begged Sarah for her forgiveness of his recent stupid and mean behavior.

He told Sarah that he adored her, promised he would never again do the dumb things he had done while they were apart, and he would never raise the subject of her religious faith or criticize her for it again if she would please forgive him and become his wife.

He also gave in to Sarah's previous uncompromising position about their being married in the church, and tearfully said to her that he would go along with any kind of wedding she wanted and wherever she wanted it to take place, regardless of their opposing personal beliefs about religious matters…if she would only become his wife because he dearly loved her with all his heart and wanted to spend the rest of his life with her.

With a teary smile on her beautiful face, Sarah hugged Tim and immediately forgave him. He then kissed her and gently slipped the engagement ring back on her finger. With happy smiles, they hurriedly set about in putting their wedding plan together in near record time while both of them were again feeling so happy and motivated towards each other, and agreed that they would be married at St. Thomas Episcopal Church as soon as possible and before their internships at the Cumberland County Regional Medical Center were to begin in the coming month.

Early the next day, Tim went to the tattoo parlor where he had gotten the tacky tattoo just two days before, and had it redone into a small flower arrangement with Sarah's name in the middle.

Chapter Four

The wedding took place only two weeks later at the historic old St. Thomas Episcopal Church, the church to which several generations of Tim's and Sarah's families had belonged. It was held on a perfectly beautiful, warm, and clear Saturday at high noon and, despite the short notice, the beautifully decorated old church was filled to its capacity with their family members and many friends.

The wedding was set to be an absolutely beautiful storybook like event. Sarah was gorgeous in her lovely white lace wedding gown, long curly blonde hair, and a veil over her beautiful face. Tim's sister, Amelia, was also beautifully attired in a pretty lavender satin gown as she served as the maid of honor from her wheelchair; Tim's Dad served as his best man, and his Mom sang a lovely solo of the beautiful old hymn, *Bless This House*.

But as lovely as his dear mother's singing voice was, nearly every word of the beautiful old hymn she was singing only served to annoy Tim deep inside, because they went directly against his still very sensitive and hardened atheistic beliefs. To further add to his ire, and unbeknown to him, Sarah's parents had arranged beforehand with the priest to have the serving of Holy Communion included as a part of the wedding ceremony.

Tim hadn't been aware of the plan to serve Holy Communion until just prior to the beginning of the wedding ceremony, and when he became aware of this, he tensed up and whispered his angry resentment over it to his father through clinched teeth about Sarah and her family's making this arrangement without first discussing it with him.

He told his Dad that they know good and well how strong he still felt about all of that phony church stuff and they had really pissed him off by slipping this communion baloney into the wedding ceremony. He said that he only agreed with Sarah that they would be married in the church, but he didn't agree to include what he referred to as "this communion bull crap." His father winced upon hearing this angry reaction from Tim, but knew better than to respond to it.

Once the ceremony had begun, Tim had no choice but to go through the motions of participating in the serving of Holy Communion rather than make an inappropriate scene by not doing so; but from that point on and throughout the remainder of the wedding ceremony, he wore an annoyed frown on his face. There was no joy in his heart, as he had suddenly lapsed into a very irritated, pouty, and aloof frame of mind.

After the wedding ceremony was over and the new bride and groom had departed from the church in a fancy chauffeur driven limousine to go to the wedding reception at the Fayetteville Highland Country Club, Tim leaned over to Sarah and showed her the communion bread wafer that had been handed to him during the service by the priest, and which he had slipped under his coat sleeve rather than ingesting it while in the church.

With a hard scowl on his face, Tim held the communion wafer directly in front of Sarah's face and angrily told her that she and her parents had better never try to trick him like that again with that phony church bull crap.

He then threw the communion wafer out of the limousine window and shouted to Sarah that this is what he thought of "that damned, rotten church's so-called body of Christ" and added that "the birds or rats would probably get more out of consuming it than he would have."

Sarah said nothing in reply, but angrily and tearfully pulled away from him, and stiffened in her resentment towards him for what he had done with the communion wafer and had said to her. The remainder of the ride from the church to the country club for the wedding reception was then as quiet and cold as the inside of a refrigerator, with both of them sitting as far apart from one other as they could, frowning, pouting, and neither looking at nor saying a single word to the other.

Just before they arrived at the country club for the wedding reception, Sarah wiped away her tears, refreshed her makeup, and pulled herself together. Then, when they arrived at the country club, she gracefully emerged from the limousine as the smiling and happy bride that she was expected to be, and Tim put on the feigned happy and smiling face expected of a groom on his wedding day.

The elegant wedding reception then proceeded as a happy event, lasting for about three hours with great live music, fun, dancing, a delicious meal, the cutting of a beautiful three tiered wedding cake, the opening of gifts, and lots of positive social interacting with their families and many friends. Once the reception was over, the anger they had felt towards each other earlier over the Holy Communion episode had finally subsided.

They then left the country club, got into their automobile, and headed south on Interstate 95 for a weeklong honeymoon at a luxurious beachfront hotel on the quaint and beautiful Tybee Island, Georgia, located on the Atlantic Ocean about eighteen miles east of the historical city of Savannah.

From that point on and throughout their week-long happy honeymoon, the inflammatory topic of their opposing religious attitudes was carefully avoided by both of them. They enjoyed a very relaxing week together tanning in the sun on the beautiful island's white sandy beach, swimming in the ocean, and walking around the island hand-in-hand as they discussed their forthcoming internships and future plans in life.

The highlight of their happy honeymoon was in the joyfully surrendering of their virginity to one another as they enjoyed their first marital intimacy with lots of pleasurable, romantic, and exciting love making!

* * * * * *

When their happy honeymoon week finally came to an end, Sarah and Tim packed their luggage into the automobile and began the five-hour drive back home to Dumont. They had to hurry back home in order to prepare for their internships, which were scheduled to begin at the Cumberland County Regional Medical Center in only twelve days.

Upon entering onto the heavily traveled Interstate 95 North highway just outside of Savannah during a sudden severe thunderstorm, they encountered a huge traffic pileup from multiple collisions that had occurred ahead of them and, as they sat in their car, a large tractor/trailer loaded with bricks slammed into the rear of their automobile, totally destroying it and badly injuring both of them.

Back in Dumont, Tim's parents saw the enormous number of accidents being covered on the NBC morning news and had feelings of anxiety because they had just spoken to Tim only an hour before the accident was reported on the news and they feared for Tim and Sarah's safety.

Sarah and Tim were both taken to the Savannah General Hospital in an ambulance. Sarah had suffered several fractured ribs, a dislocated shoulder, a badly sprained ankle, and several minor bruises and lacerations. Although in intense pain, she was lucid and appeared to be in no grave or life-threatening danger from her injuries.

Tim, however, had fallen into a deep coma from having received several severe traumas to his head and had to be placed on life support in the hospital's intensive care unit. The physician in charge of the case had expressed serious doubts that Tim would ever recover from his comatose state.

When they received the terrible news from the hospital, Sarah's and Tim's parents and Tim's younger sister, Amelia, immediately drove down to Savannah to be with them during this tragic and difficult time. Even the church's priest, Reverend Roberts and his lovely wife, Patty, drove down to Savannah to show their caring and support for Sarah, Tim and their families.

Both of their parents, along with Amelia and Sarah, who sat beside Tim's bed in their wheelchairs, constantly remained with him in the intensive care unit, and took turns holding his limp hand while they steadily prayed around the clock for his recovery.

As they were saying their nearly continuous prayers, begging God to spare Tim's life, Sarah said to Amelia, "It sure is a mighty good thing that Tim can't hear us saying our prayers to God for him like we are or he would probably be very annoyed!" Unbeknownst to them, Tim was able to hear every word they were saying and he was very annoyed, but unable to express his annoyance.

After nearly two days of being in a deep comatose state in the intensive care unit, the loud beeping alarm of the several monitors that were attached to Tim's body suddenly began to sound. He could initially hear them, but they then soon began to fade off into the distance as he felt himself floating free of his body and drifting down into what appeared to be a long, fog-filled and dark tunnel.

Sarah and the others began to weep because they knew what the monitoring alarms were probably indicating…that Tim was dying. Upon hearing the sound of the alarms, the nurse and a doctor immediately rushed into the room and, after examining Tim's vital signs, he was officially pronounced as dead.

* * * * * *

Tim was unaware of what was happening in the hospital as he continued to feel himself floating free from his body and further down the heavily fog filled tunnel, and he eventually saw a nearly blinding bright white light glowing further ahead of him. When he reached the light, he heard some soft and beautiful music playing that sounded almost like the kind of music he used to hear when he was in church.

What then followed was a major life-changing experience for Tim, and one for which he would forever remember every single detail.

He heard a friendly voice say to him, "Welcome, Tim; we're glad to have you join us. Please come along and follow me, and I'll be serving as your guide while you are here."

Tim was confused by what was happening, and asked where he was and who the voice was that was speaking to him.

The voice replied, "You are in Heaven, Tim, and my name is Gabriel. I've been given the honor of greeting and guiding you around here, where you will meet a lot of good people from your past Earthly life that have loved and missed seeing you since their coming here to Heaven, and I know they will be delighted to be able to visit with you again. There are also many of your ancestors whom you will be meeting for the first time and, most important of all, Tim, later on you will have a private meeting with our Lord Jesus Christ."

Although Gabriel had no visible Earthly physical form, Tim was able to clearly hear him and perceived his presence as being kind and friendly, so he followed behind him down the now clear pathway that was filled with many bright and beautiful colors.

Tim was happily surprised when his departed grandfather suddenly appeared and welcomed him…but without a body or any visible physical characteristics; yet, strangely, Tim was immediately aware of his presence and was elated to be reunited with his dear grandfather who had been his very best friend during his earlier childhood days.

Although his grandfather wasn't in a physical human form as Tim remembered him, Tim could recognize his beloved grandfather's familiar voice speaking to him.

"Tim, my dear grandson, you can't imagine how happy I am to be with you again. I sure did enjoy those many wonderful times in our former lives that we shared when we used to go fishing and play golf together back on Earth. You're going to really enjoy being in this fantastic place far more than anything you've ever before known; and, my good little buddy, you'll be glad to know that, thanks to our dear Father, God, I no longer use cigarettes because they don't have any of those nasty things here that I know you used to despise my smoking when we were back on Earth!"

After several minutes of a happy reunion and chatting had been shared between Tim and his grandfather, Gabriel politely interrupted them and said, "I know you two fellows are so happy to be with each other again, but you're going to have to cut it a little short for now because Tim has a pretty busy schedule to keep while he's here. He's going to meet a few of his other relatives, and then he will have a very important meeting in the garden with our dear Lord, Jesus Christ."

Tim asked Gabriel if there really was such a person as Jesus Christ.

Gabriel said, "Yes, Tim, there most certainly is and no greater person has ever existed. I know you're going to immediately love Him like we all do; but before you have your important meeting with Him, I will let you spend a few more minutes with some of your other ancestors who also want to visit with you, and I'm sure you will all enjoy being with each other."

Tim then spent a short while visiting with his grandfather and grandmother whom he had known several years ago before they died, his great and great-great grandparents, and other long ago deceased members of his family about whom he had heard many wonderful things from his mother and father, and whose pictures he had seen in the old family photograph album but whom he had never met in person. It was a joyful meeting, and all of them were glowing with pleasure!

Chapter Five

After Tim had enjoyed the happy reunion with his grandparents and several of his other never before met ancestors, and was beginning to feel the very best he had in his entire life, Gabriel said, "Okay, Tim, we will head on over to the garden now and you will meet our wonderful leader, our Lord Jesus Christ, who's been expecting you. Are you looking forward to your meeting with Him?"

Tim told Gabriel that he was but was very nervous about it.

Gabriel assured Tim that he had nothing to fear, and then led him into a bright and beautifully colored garden where Jesus, who radiated a warm, glowing, and exceptionally strong presence, greeted him.

Jesus spoke to Tim in a gentle and friendly voice. "Greetings and welcome to Heaven, Tim! I'm so pleased that we are finally getting to personally meet and have a chat together. My name is Jesus and I've heard some mighty interesting things about you and your many impressive accomplishments while you were back on Earth.

But I do have to tell you, Tim, that it has been kind of disheartening to me when someone as intelligent and otherwise as good a person as you clearly are have claimed that you don't believe in me or our Father…like we never even existed according to you and your Atheist friends; and that you also regard our wonderful and important church that we established long ago in order to help humankind by teaching our people how to live a better life as being an evil and fraudulent institution as well."

Feeling awed by Jesus's presence and deeply ashamed of his past faulty thinking, Tim apologetically said to Jesus that since he now had the experience of being there in Heaven only briefly and had the honor of meeting Him and knowing that He really does exist, that view he once held about those things had immediately and completely gone away from his mind, and he humbly apologized to Jesus for his past incorrect beliefs.

Tim told Jesus that he hoped He would find it in His heart to forgive him for his inappropriate behavior and his former ignorance-based views about Him, our Father, God, and the church they had established to help educate their people.

From that moment on, Tim would remember every single word that Jesus said to him for the rest of his life. They would forever remain indelibly etched in his brain!

Jesus said, "You needn't put yourself down and your apology is not necessary, Tim, but I do accept it, my friend and brother. I understand that you've been struggling for a long time with a lot of issues involving Heaven, me, the soul, and our Father, God, as many people on Earth unfortunately do. I'll be glad to help clear them up for you, and I believe it will result in a changing of your thinking about those very important matters."

Tim told Jesus that he been very confused about those things for a long time, and admitted that he was obviously wrong about what he had thought and said about those very important things during the period that he claimed to be an Atheist. Tim humbly asked Jesus if he should address Him as his Lord and Savior, like they would address Him as being if they were in the church, which Tim admitted that he had also so stupidly and wrongly criticized and rejected.

Jesus replied in a warm and friendly voice, "Hey, young fellow, please just relax and enjoy your visit here because you never have to feel afraid of or beholden to me. I want you to feel free to call me by whatever name makes you comfortable, because I've been called just about everything from a carpenter to a prophet, and even an imposter or one who never even existed by some people, but such things really don't matter to me.

I was finally referred to as the Son of God and the Lord and Savior of mankind by my Earthly Christian-believing church and most of our Father's children, so I can handle just about any name or title that's thrown at me, Tim, whether they're critical or complimentary. Titles were never a big thing to me anyhow because they are only words, and it's what one truly believes and what they do in their lives that really matters to our Father and me much more than by what they say.

Contrary to what you may have been accustomed to hearing about me, Tim, although the circumstances and conditions of my human birth and life back on Earth were quite different from yours in many ways, I'm still a regular guy just like you and I'm not big on self-adoration, titles, or any of those grandiose words to which you may have heard me being referred. Frankly, Tim, those pathetic narcissistic people who thrive on and hide behind their pompous and often undeserved titles and roles have always bored me!

And by the way, Tim, since we're not in my wonderful church on Earth right now, where communications are sometimes much more on the formal side, you can drop those thee's, thou's, arts, and other antiquated sounding language forms like they often use there, too. You or just plain old Jesus, and ordinary straight talk between two decent and caring guys will work just fine for me! After all, we both have the same ultimate Father who created and exists within all of us, so that makes us brothers, doesn't it?"

Tim mumbled, "Yes, sir, it does make wonderful sense to me now that you put it that way" as he felt both deeply humbled and blessed. Before him was the greatest person to ever walk on the face of the Earth; the one whom many generations of people had placed on a pedestal and worshipped for the many centuries after His perfect earthly life, crucifixion, death, and resurrection.

Tim was beside himself with amazement that he was actually having a friendly conversation with Jesus like He was just a regular guy…a kindly and *real friend* and brother, instead of the nonexistent and fictional person that Tim had previously perceived Him as being while he claimed to be an Atheist, but who had now suddenly and completely changed his thinking!

The words to the hymns that he had learned many years ago when he was a small child and attended Sunday school came into his mind; *What a Friend We Have in Jesus, Fairest Lord Jesus, and Jesus Loves Me;* and Tim immediately perceived Him as such, his very best, bravest, and most caring friend ever!

Jesus continued by saying, "The only relationship I want you and I to have with each other, Tim, is for us to be real good *friends* and I would like to become your best and most caring and trusted friend forever if you are ready and willing to accept me as such.

I don't expect you and I to always see eye-to-eye on everything, Tim, because our Father gave all of us individual personalities and free wills that are unique to each of us, and our personal views and preferences may not always be completely congruent on the less important matters.

But there are some very important basic things about which you need to know and always apply if you want to get the most out of your Earthly life and the eternal one here which will follow it.

When our Father decided that humankind needed one of their own to teach and help them to learn the best way to live their lives on Earth, He had me conceived by my blessed and beautiful Mother, Mary, through the power of His Holy Spirit so that He could live through me when I was born on Earth to live the life of an Earthly being.

He directed me to teach and set an example for all of his children to follow in order that they might learn the way to experience a more rewarding life while they are on Earth, and become better educated and prepared to someday reside here in Heaven with Him to enjoy an even greater life for all of eternity.

It sure wasn't an easy journey for me while I was in my human form back on Earth, but I obeyed our Father's will as I always did, so I could satisfy the very important mission on Earth for which He had me created.

It was especially tough when our Father eventually allowed and even arranged for me to suffer a miserable death on the cross at a place on Earth called Calvary in order to convey an important example and set of messages that would be of help to all of humankind in the future by encouraging them to lead the right kind of life through my living example while on Earth, regardless of the circumstances and conditions…a life that would better prepare them for the eternal one here that would follow.

And, Tim, believe me when I tell you that the pain of having those large nails driven into my hands and feet, having an ugly and painful crown of thorns stuck onto my scalp to humiliate me and what I stood for, and then having my side sliced open by a Roman soldier was awful more than you can imagine. Believe me, I felt the pain just as badly as you or anyone else on Earth would, and it sure did hurt something awful!

But I knew down deep inside my soul that I had to comply with our Father's mission for me, in spite of the terribly torturous physical and mental pain it was causing me. He knew what future generations of humankind needed to know and what my role in it had to be. Well, that pretty much sums up my whole story in a nutshell, Tim. Now tell me what questions I may answer to help you?"

Tim then told Jesus that his first and most troubling question had to do with our Father, God. He asked Jesus if God really exists, was the creator of the universe and, if so, would he ever be able to see Him. Those were among the many things he used to wonder a lot about before he took up his Atheism where he didn't believe in much of anything that couldn't be proven to him.

Jesus replied, "That's an interesting question, Tim, and it's one that most folks will never be able to fully comprehend. Our Father, God, certainly does exist. In fact, He's in every square inch of the universe and is so awesome, powerful, and mighty that no one has ever actually seen Him in a single humanlike form, which is why He had me created, and He is always with us through me and through His powerful and invisible Holy Spirit.

Many Earthly artists in the past have painted their perception of our Father, God, as being a kindly, frail-looking, graying, and balding old man with a long white beard and a glowing halo hanging over His head, but that's not our wonderful Father…He's so much more than that, Tim. In fact, as we speak, He's here inside both of us and in the garden that surrounds us, and He exists throughout the entire universe.

Our Father, God, is *everywhere,* Tim, but I must tell you that neither I nor anyone else could ever be able to adequately describe in human terms or even begin to fully comprehend one as omnipotent, loving, powerful, ubiquitous, and completely perfect in every conceivable way as our Creator and dear Father, God, is."

Tim said to Jesus that what He just told him was really heavy and difficult for him to even imagine! He said that he also couldn't understand how neither of them has a body resembling those like the ones they had back on Earth; yet they are able to see, recognize, and communicate with each other even though they don't even have eyes to see, ears to hear, or mouths with which to speak. This all seemed so strange to Tim, so he asked Jesus if He would please explain that one for him.

Jesus replied, "Not a problem, Tim. You see, we are all basically souls, and souls are the intangible and the very uniquely essence of all human beings from the moment we are born into our temporary Earthly bodies. Our souls are somewhat like what has been described by some of the earlier Earthly scholars such as Aristotle and Plato as being the same as our psyches, and our souls are more uniquely personal than the fingerprints on the bodies which we temporarily occupied while on Earth but now no longer need any more than the clothes we once wore.

And these souls will continue living on forever, Tim; even after our temporary Earthly bodies wear out, die, rot in the ground, and then turn to dust. Yet, as you have already noticed, we are still able to recognize and communicate with one another even better than we ever could before when we were limited to our physical bodies.

That's pretty much how things work here in Heaven, Tim...no bodies, just souls; but souls that are always very comfortable, never experience pain, are always completely happy, and are more uniquely different from one another than the physical bodies that contained them while on the Earth.

And behaviorally, Tim, there are three basic things that our souls never experience here in Heaven, but are unfortunately pretty common with many of the folks back on Earth and they all begin with an A. We never experience *anger* towards one another for any reason, for it is the most dangerous and destructive of all the mental dysfunctions experienced by and between mortals; nor *anxiety,* which is irrational fear, because we never have to be afraid of anything here in Heaven; nor *arrogance*, which is placing oneself above another. Here in Heaven, we are all happy, contented, confident, and completely love one another. Do you understand that, Tim?"

Tim told Jesus that it made great sense and he was beginning to see His point. He said that he recognized his grandfather from the moment that he, without any eyes to see, saw him even though his grandfather had no human body like Tim remembered him as having when he was alive back on Earth, and everyone he had met there seemed so happy and content. Tim said to Jesus that this was all really so strange but so absolutely wonderful to him.

Jesus said, "These things may seem strange to you now, Tim, but people here in Heaven get used to and happily adjust to those changes in their being pretty quickly after they arrive here. Do you have any more questions to ask of me?"

Tim said that he did, and it had been one of the many things that troubled him for a long time. He said that when he was living on Earth just about everyone he knew said their prayers to Him and our Father, God, from when they first awakened each morning, before they ate all of their meals, and before they went to sleep at night…practically all of the time.

He asked Jesus how could He or our Father, God, possibly listen to the probably many millions of people that talked to them all at once several times every day, and how could they still accurately process all of their individual messages and then quickly give them back the helpful responses that they sought from them. He said that this whole process seemed completely impossible to him.

Jesus replied, "Then let me explain it to you in a way that might help to make it a little easier for you to understand. You are familiar with computers, aren't you Tim?"

Tim said he was and that he even had one himself.

Jesus continued by asking, "And aren't some of those larger computers capable of processing millions of complex transactions at the same time and handling all of them with a pretty high level of speed and efficiency?"

Tim replied that he understood them to be very capable of doing that.

Jesus then said, "Then doesn't it make sense to you, Tim, that our Father who created the entire universe, including all of those smart people who designed the computers, would be able to do everything and even much more in the processing of our people's prayers than a simple man-made computer could do?"

Tim said that it really did make good sense to him when Jesus explained it in that more understandable way. He told Jesus that another thing that sort of confused him was that he hears God and His universe often referred to as having neither a beginning nor an end; yet, everything he had ever known in his Earthly life has always had both a beginning and an end to it, especially including their mortal lives. He asked if Jesus could please clarify that one for him.

Jesus said, "Sure, Tim; envision a circle and tell me where it begins and where it ends. It has neither a beginning nor an end, and it goes on forever doesn't it? That's the simplest description I can give you of the universe and eternity. Only our Father and those of us who permanently reside here are capable of fully understanding what eternity is all about, and you will eventually begin to better understand this after you've been here longer. Is there anything else on your mind that I can clear up for you?"

Tim then asked Jesus what about those no-good and evil people who committed many really serious sins while in their Earthly lives and if they were also allowed to be in Heaven with Him and our Father.

Jesus replied, "The answer is yes and no, Tim. Most people will be forgiven of their sins by our Father when they sincerely repent of them and ask our Father for His forgiveness; but just talk alone won't get the job done if they aren't sincere and don't walk in the right way after they have been forgiven. Afterwards, if their walk is right, their souls are cleansed of their sins and they will enjoy their Earthly life more and will fit here in Heaven very nicely.

The really evil ones, though; people like Adolf Hitler, Charles Manson, serial murderers, and those fortunately few other deeply evil and unrepentant people never could make it past their mortal lives and into Heaven because their chronically wicked behavior on Earth has actually destroyed their souls beyond repair even before their physical demise occurred, and they just wouldn't fit in here in Heaven without a soul.

They are essentially totally evil, like Satan, and when their soul destroyed bodies finally die they actually do completely cease to exist and turn to dust as your atheist friends believe will happen to everyone, and they miss out on the joy of being here in Heaven forever."

Tim then asked Jesus what the deal was about that terrible place that people call Hell, as he had been led to believe that all of the really bad people have to go there to suffer some terribly miserable punishment for all of eternity after they die.

Jesus replied, "I'm glad you asked me about that one, Tim, because many people on Earth still don't really have a correct understanding of what Hell is all about, and some beliefs tend to sometimes go a little overboard on the Hell thing; but there's no such place as a Hell after mortal life ends. It's because our deeply loving Father wouldn't want any of His children whom He created to suffer such a torturous misery as Hell is described as being, no matter how evil they were.

Some people, however, do experience a form of what you could call Hell while they are still living their Earthly lives as a consequence of the bad choices they made with their God-given free wills. These bad choices are most often extreme violations of our Father's basic guidelines for a good life that He spelled out in the Ten Commandments which He gave to His children in stone tablets through Moses…and this is often referred to by some with the expression that you've probably heard called a Hell on Earth."

Tim then said that there are so many different religious denominations that interpret—or misinterpret—things so differently, and asked Jesus which religious denomination was the most correct one for people on Earth to follow.

Jesus replied, "Tim, they are all basically good, and the main differences between them are largely in the manner or style in which they choose to learn about and worship our God and, most of all, how they live their lives. When you go above the steeple line of all the churches, temples, synagogues, and other places of study and worship, regardless of their architecture, language, or style of worship, they are all basically on the same track about the most important things, which is fundamentally the way in which they live their lives and interact with others.

For example, Tim, my Roman Catholic, Anglican, Lutheran, and Jewish friends, and some other religious groups are more formally structured in their beautiful style of worship than others, and many of them are less formal; but that part makes none any better or less than the other. They are all good people, including many of my brothers and sisters of some other religious beliefs.

Some of them don't even know of me or our Father, or haven't yet chosen to accept me as the Messiah. But most of them are still very good people in the eyes of our Father and me. Believing in our Father and me, regardless of what name you choose to call us, is very important and helpful, but what you do in your life is of even far more importance to us.

There are some people who, for various reasons, haven't had the benefit of knowing enough about us; yet the Holy Spirit is still operating inside their souls and directs them to live as our father, God, wants them to. A little over a hundred years ago, an Earthly psychiatrist named Dr. Sigmund Freud in Austria came close to describing the Holy Spirit's role when he presented the concept of a super ego, or conscience, as being a built-in moral compass which helps guide people in their daily moral decision-making.

Our Father, God, is always kind and loving, and is not intentionally mean to any of His children. He doesn't want to cause them to suffer any kind of pain...but you're either in Heaven or you're not, and you're either one of His or you're not; and there's no in-between. Do you have any more questions to ask of me, Tim?"

Tim told Jesus that there were none that he could think of at the moment, and that this had been such an enlightening experience for him.

Then it occurred to Tim that he did have a final question to ask, a really important one. He said that when he first arrived in Heaven, his guide, Gabriel, had given him the impression that he was only visiting there in Heaven and that He, Jesus, had also given him the same impression that he may soon be returning back to his Earthly life.

He asked Jesus if this was so, why was he allowed to have this wonderful and enlightening experience with Him, and if he would have to leave that beautiful place. He said that he really loved being with Jesus and the others, and would like to stay there forever if He would allow him to, even though he would have to miss and wait for his dear wife, Sarah, to join him after her Earthly life was over.

Jesus replied, "You have been temporarily summoned here, Tim, because our Father and I have selected you and a few special other high quality people to serve as potential new kinds of messengers of the truth on the Earth; but not in being preachers of the Gospel, although they have always served a very important spiritual leadership and teaching role.

There are already many mighty good ones of those on Earth; very fine people like my friends, Billy Graham, the Popes, rabbis, and many others, including the minister of your own church, Reverend Allen Roberts. Unfortunately, though, people who are like you once were made the wrong choice by not listening to what they had to tell you, and by not respecting or believing them.

That is where you will fit into our plan, Tim; through your living example and commitment to living by our Father, God's, principles or, as the saying goes, by 'walking the talk'. Then, even some of those hardened non-believers like you once were will probably get the message and many will change the way in which they live their lives for the better by emulating the way in which you live yours. You have been blessed by our Father with the gift of a very high level of human intelligence, a great personality, and many other advantages to make good use of."

Jesus said He hoped that Tim now had sufficient and understandable answers to some of the questions that have disturbed him since he was a child and had caused him to abandon his Christian faith and embrace Atheism. He asked Tim if he had any more questions to ask of Him.

Tim told Jesus there were none that he could think of at the moment and that the great information that He had thus far so kindly shared with him had already enlightened him with a one hundred and eighty degree different view about the most important things in his life.

Jesus replied, "You will probably have more questions as you travel further down the road of your Earthly life, Tim, and you will be able to get most of the answers you seek from reading the book of knowledge that was created by our Father called the Holy Bible, or through communicating directly with us through prayer."

Tim asked if Jesus meant that the Bible was really totally factual because even that never made a lot of sense to him either, since he understood that it was supposedly written long ago by a lot of different human beings in many different forms, times, circumstances, and places and translated into many languages.

Jesus said, "Yes the Holy Bible is absolutely true, Tim…it's the real thing. It's loaded with absolutely pure fact, and is sort of like a human operator's manual which largely focuses upon relationships with everyone from your parents, siblings, spouses, children, neighbors, strangers, your friends, and even your enemies, and on up to and including your relationship with our Father and me…and how to live with all of them in the most rewarding and peaceful way.

Although it was penned by mortals and has often been misunderstood or misinterpreted by some, the Holy Bible was inspired and guided by our Father through His Holy Spirit for the human writers to document, and all the truths in it from the day they were written are still applicable today and will remain so forever, even though some have difficulty in understanding and often misinterpret some of its metaphors and analogies.

When you are confronted with any questions about most of life's issues, you will find virtually all of the answers contained in His book. As an example of one of many you should always keep in mind is in the Book that was penned by Matthew, my old pal while I was on Earth. In chapter 28, verse 20, it says *I am with you always*, and that's a fact, Tim…I am and will always be with you.

All you have to do is speak to me and I will hear and transmit my responses back to your mind on any issue you might have, 24/7/365. Just say your prayer; then pause and patiently listen with a clear and open mind, and you will quickly receive my response into your mind. It's really very simple and has worked well for many billions of people for over two thousand years!"

Jesus then said, "Now that you're on the team with us, Tim, how would you like to take an interesting tour with me before you return back to your life on Earth? We can take a quick spin together around some really interesting places on the Earth and elsewhere that you've never before seen if you'd like. It's something that I often do and I know you will also enjoy."

Tim told Him that he would like that and asked how they would do it.

Jesus said, "I'll get us a couple of doves and we'll cruise around on them. It's always been my favorite way to travel when I go down for a visit to the Earth, which I often do, and where I've also even taken the form of a pathetic human street beggar or another needy person on occasion to encourage the kindness and love of my brothers and sisters towards such unfortunate people."

Two pure white doves then suddenly appeared before them and Jesus said, "Hop on one of these little birds, Tim, and we'll head out on our grand tour."

Jesus and Tim then flew down to the Earth together on the doves, and the flight was the most incredibly spectacular and enjoyable adventure, and unlike anything that Tim had ever experienced. They rapidly glided close to several other planets and then down to Earth over forests, down valleys, across oceans and rivers, past cities, over mountains, and finally landed on a window ledge on the outside of the Savannah General Hospital. Tim could see Sarah sitting in her wheelchair and looking out of her hospital room window, and she could see the two white doves through her tear-filled eyes.

Jesus smiled and said, "Let's you and I do a few loop-de-loops on the birds in front of your Sarah's window, Tim. That'll help to lift her spirits a little bit because she really could use something different and cheerful like that to give her grieving mind a little distraction from some of the sadness she's probably feeling from thinking that she will never see you again."

Tim told Jesus that it was mighty nice of Him to think of doing that for her and asked when he might be going back into his human form.

Jesus replied, "You'll be back inside your Earthly body within the hour, Tim, and I must warn you that you'll initially have a brief but pretty bad hangover from your previous physical injuries; but I assure you that both you and Sarah will then get completely well quickly afterwards."

Tim thanked Jesus, his new and best friend forever, for all He had done for him and again asked why He had called for him to be in His presence because he thought he might not ever return to Earth.

He replied, "I arranged for it to happen because you needed to be here to see that we're for real and your church is not, as you had previously chosen to believe, a bunch of phonies who are only seeking to gain control of its peoples' minds and money. And, as I told you before, we want you to use the knowledge that you've gained here in helping others who are struggling with the same problem that you once did; not by your talk, but by your upright *walk*."

Jesus then told Tim that, as a little farewell gift from the visit with Him in Heaven, He was going to make his little sister, Amelia, completely well from her earlier injuries and that Tim would see the process of her healing beginning to happen pretty soon after his return to North Carolina, and it will amaze her good doctors who won't be able to understand or explain how it happened.

Tim happily thanked Him, his dear brother and savior, for doing something so very wonderful for her and said this great news was a beautiful gift that he deeply appreciated and knew she would love!

Jesus said, "You are most welcome and remember, Tim, as I told you before, you will help others find the right way to live by being a living example; a role model for them to follow in the way that you walk rather than by talking about what you now know.

And by the way, Tim, if you should tell anyone too much about the experience you had while you were here with me in Heaven, some might think that you're crazy as a loon and have you locked up in an insane asylum, and then you'd not be able to perform the important mission we have planned for you!"

Tim again apologized to Jesus, telling Him that he was so very sorry for the way he had been, because until he actually met Him he really didn't know any better. He said he had been so frustrated and confused by it all, and now realized that he had taken the path of least resistance by running away from it instead of trying harder to understand and embrace it…and that, in some ways, he felt that he was even worse to Jesus with his own past behavior than Judas had been when he betrayed Jesus.

Jesus replied, "Well, now you do know the absolute truth, Tim, and you are completely forgiven of all your past sins of ignorance. I hope you will put the knowledge that you've gained here to a good use, my brother, and start *walking the talk*; and I look forward to seeing you again one day further down the road as one of my good and permanent neighbors here in Heaven. Goodbye, my brother."

Jesus hugged Tim, spiritually, reminded him again of the quote from the Bible in the Book of Matthew, waved a friendly goodbye to him, and then disappeared up into the sky on His white dove.

Chapter Six

A long black hearse with two men from a Cumberland County funeral home slowly pulled up and parked in front of the hospital emergency room entrance. It had been sent to the hospital to transport Tim's body back home for preparation and burial. A hospital security guard led the two men to the morgue who were pulling a gurney with a plastic body bag and casket on it into which Tim's body was to be placed.

After the two men from the funeral home opened the heavy morgue door, they pulled back the sheet that was covering Tim in order to place his body into the bag and into the casket. They were shocked to see him suddenly sit up on the gurney with a wide grin on his face!

Tim asked the men what in the world took them so long to get there and jokingly told them he had been practically freezing his tail off while he had been kept locked up in that cold and dark place for nearly an entire day while waiting for them to show up.

The security guard fainted and fell to the floor from the shock of seeing Tim alive, and the two men from the funeral home went running wildly down the hospital hall in sheer terror, screaming "He's alive!"

When the news of Tim's return to life reached Sarah, who had been in a deep state of depression and was sitting alone in her room in a wheelchair, she quickly jumped out of the wheelchair and excitedly raced down the hall.

She knocked over a cart and pushed people out of her way, was barefoot and clad only in her skimpy hospital gown, and ignored the pain from running on her sprained ankle to get to where Tim was standing in the hallway waiting for her with a warm smile on his face and his arms open wide.

Tim said to her with a happy smile, "I'm back home, Honey!" and then lifted her up into his arms and tightly hugged her.

"Oh thank you God, thank you so much my dear God!" Sarah shouted through her happy tears as she jumped up and down with delirious joy. As he held Sarah close to him, Tim looked straight into her tear-filled, happy eyes and warmly said to her, "Yes, my dear, beautiful and wonderful wife, you are so right…we really should give thanks to our great and loving God that we're finally back together again." To Sarah, this was such a strange statement to hear coming from the mouth of Tim the previously hardened non-believer, but she gladly accepted it without any question or further comment.

The hospital staff was amazed and shocked at Tim's return to life. A local television reporter had heard about Tim's return from death and asked him for an interview, which Tim politely chose to decline because his newly discovered purpose in life was to walk the talk and not just talk it!

* * * * * *

After they had spent only two more days in the hospital, to the amazement of their doctors, Sarah and Tim had both quickly and completely healed from their injuries and were considered well enough to be discharged.

Their automobile insurance company had made a quick settlement in the total loss of their previously wrecked car, and they purchased a brand new Jeep Grand Cherokee in Savannah before beginning their return trip to Fayetteville where they were still scheduled to start their internship duties at the Cumberland County Regional Medical Center on the day after returning home.

As they were riding north on Interstate Highway 95 on a clear and sunny day and had just crossed the South Carolina State Line, Sarah asked Tim, "Honey, would you please share something with me that's been weighing heavily on my mind if you are able to?"

Tim told her that he would be glad to tell her whatever she wanted to know if he could.

She asked him to please explain what is was like when he was unconscious and, as she and the doctors thought, was physically dead. She said that she couldn't even imagine what it would be like to be in such a deep coma as he was in and asked if he could recall anything at all about it.

Tim smiled and told her that he sure could recall a whole lot about it and could honestly tell her that it was an absolutely *heavenly* experience for him. He added that, although he may have appeared to be completely out of it to her, the doctors, and the monitoring instruments that were connected to him while he was in that deep coma, he was very conscious, internally, and it was definitely a real life-changing experience for him.

Sarah asked, "In what way could something as dangerous and scary as that coma you were in have been be a life-changing experience for you?"

He told her that, while he was out of it in the normal conscious and physical sense, he internally gained some very deep insights about some extremely important issues pertaining to his beliefs that had been very troubling to him ever since he was a little boy, and things that had nearly messed up his life as recently as just a few weeks ago. He asked Sarah if she could guess what they were. Sarah replied, "I don't have a clue as to what you could be talking about, Honey, so please explain it to me."

Tim then pulled their Jeep off of the highway and into the parking lot of the South Carolina State Welcome and Rest area, where he stopped and shut off the engine. He then turned toward Sarah, held both of her hands in his, looked directly into her eyes, and told her that while he may have appeared to be dead to her, from his experience he had become and shall forever remain a true believer in and will follow our Father, God, and His Son, our Lord and Savior, Jesus Christ… that Jesus will be his very best friend for the rest of his life; and that he didn't just believe it, he knew it to be so and he intended to do all in his power to walk in His footsteps until He calls him to be home with Him forever in that wonderful place he had recently visited called Heaven!

"Wow!" shouted Sarah in a choking voice and with happy tears streaming down her cheeks. "Do you really mean what you just said to me, Honey? I don't know what could have happened to you that would cause that huge of a change to occur in your mind, but hearing that wonderful statement that you just made makes you a fantastically perfect man in my mind and causes me to feel like I'm the luckiest woman in the world to be your wife!" Tim told her that he absolutely did mean every single word of it, and thanked her for the very appreciated but undeserved compliment… that she really did flatter him by thinking of him to be, as she said, 'a fantastically perfect man'; but told her that they both knew he was very far from being that, and they both also knew to whom that title only really belongs…to our Lord and Savior, Jesus Christ.

He promised Sarah that when they got back home and his head became a little bit clearer, he would try to explain the whole story to her in more detail about how this incredibly wonderful epiphany had occurred to him, and that he was sure she was going to have a really hard time believing what she was going to hear when he shared it with her in more detail… and that she may even think that he had gone completely nuts. "I can't wait to hear it when you're ready to share it!" Sarah happily replied.

They warmly embraced and then resumed the trip north to Fayetteville with happy smiles on their faces. As they rode, they held hands and joyfully sang happy songs and some church hymns together that, at Tim's suggestion, included hymns he remembered from Sunday school as a small child; *What a Friend We Have in Jesus, Fairest Lord Jesus, and Jesus Loves Me!*

They finally arrived back at Tim's parents' home in Dumont later that afternoon where both of their families were eagerly waiting to greet them and celebrate Tim's return from what they had thought had been the end of his mortal life.

After a joyful and tearful reunion, Tim's parents also happily reported that Amelia's eyesight had suddenly miraculously begun improving on the day before, to the point where she didn't even need her thick reading glasses to see, and that she was beginning to feel some never before experienced tingling sensations in her lower body. She was scheduled to see her neurosurgeon and ophthalmologist in the coming days to follow up on these surprising and encouraging changes.

Tim wasn't the least bit surprised to hear this because he already knew exactly why it had happened, but didn't comment on it except to bow his head and silently say, "Thank You, my friend, Jesus, for your wonderful gift to Amelia and for always being a man of Your word."

After the joyful family gathering that was filled with lots of hugs and happy tears was finally over, Sarah and Tim got into their car and headed for home. When they arrived there, they quickly undressed, then knelt together beside their bed and said a prayer of thanksgiving together, ending with "We pray the Lord our souls to keep…Amen." They then crashed into their bed from sheer exhaustion and slept deeply through the night.

* * * * * *

Early the following morning, Sarah and Tim awakened, crawled out of bed, dressed, and drove over to the Cumberland County Regional Medical Center to report in for their first day of duty as interns.

After receiving a cordial welcome from the Hospital Administrator and his senior staff, they were given a general orientation on the policies and procedures they would be expected to follow during their approximately one year of service as interns, including information about the rather slim compensation and limited benefits. They were also each issued two white lab coats and engraved metallic hospital name tags which, to their delight, had M.D. written after their names…and seeing those two little letters alone was very special!

Then, as a routine part of the in-processing procedure, along with eight other new interns, they were sent over to the hospital's Behavioral Health Department for a routine screening and orientation by the hospital's senior staff psychiatrist, Dr. Bob Cason. Cason was a handsome, slightly portly, and very friendly man in his early seventies who had been a star football player at Duke University during his four years of undergraduate study where he majored in Theology and

Chemistry prior to attending and graduating from its medical school. Prior to joining the hospital staff, he had enjoyed many successful years of practicing psychiatry in Fayetteville.

As Dr. Cason interviewed each of the interns, he asked them to respond to a set of questions that had been designed by him to help identify any members of the group who might be in need of personal counseling or special assistance during their internship. The first question Dr. Cason asked each of the interns was: "Where do you consider yourself to be ranked among your fellow interns in terms of your medical knowledge and competencies? Do you feel that you are in the highest, middle, or lowest third?" Eight of the interns rated themselves as probably being the middle third; one rated himself in the highest, and one in the lowest third.

Dr. Cason then made a notation to schedule the two interns with non-average perceptions for further interviewing to ascertain on what grounds they based their personal assessment… fear, confidence or lack of same, competence or incompetence, or just outright arrogance or self-abasement?

The other remaining questions were also directed at determining their personal needs and issues, levels of medical knowledge, and practical judgment…but the last question he asked was quite out of the ordinary. Dr. Cason then asked each of the interns a question for which he had received previous criticism from some of his hospital colleagues for asking because many considered it to be irrelevant and inappropriate, but Cason had ignored their criticism and continued to ask it of all new interns.

He asked them, "Do you believe in God and, if so why; or if not, why not?" Seven of the interns, including Sarah, responded in the affirmative and their reasons were basically because they chose to believe. One replied in the negative and stated as his reason that he was an agnostic who was leaning towards atheism or anti-theism because he had not yet seen enough proof to believe in much of anything beyond what he could see and prove. Tim could easily relate to this intern's feelings.

A scarf-draped female intern from Syria stated that she was a Muslim and believed only in Allah, and viewed those who believed otherwise as being foolish infidels. And–you know who–Tim replied, "Yes sir, I surely do believe in our Father, God, and in His Son, Jesus Christ, who showed us the right way to live and He is my Lord, Savior, leader, and the very best friend in my life."

Tim's statement was clearly much more of a response than Dr. Cason, who was also a strongly committed and devout Christian who actively participated in the activities of Snyder Memorial Baptist Church in Fayetteville, had ever received from the question given him by any intern in the past. Dr. Cason immediately took a special personal liking towards Tim and it was mutual.

In fact, this early friendly relationship with Dr. Cason planted the first seed of thought in Tim's mind that he might want to learn more about psychiatry and maybe even give some thought about pursuing a residency in it upon the completion of his basic internship instead of the earlier choice he had expressed to do his residency in general surgery. All of the interns were then each assigned to a licensed medical staff doctor from their tentatively planned future area of medical specialty who would serve as their mentors during their basic internship, and they would be rotated for duty in each of the hospital's areas of medical service.

Tim was pleased to learn that he would be assigned under the aegis of Dr. Cason due to the fact that all of the staff surgeons were already fully committed to mentoring other interns. Sarah had chosen to pursue a career in pediatrics, and was assigned to Dr. Gene Finch who served as Chairman of the Pediatrics Department. Dr. Finch was a friendly, handsome, and very likeable man who had been born in India and who was also an actively practicing Christian at a local United Methodist church.

From a religious perspective, both Sarah and Tim couldn't have been more satisfied with their mentor assignments. At the end of their first day as interns, which had lasted for over twelve hours and included following their mentors and other specialists on rounds with patients, Sarah and Tim returned to the condo feeling nearly overwhelmed and exhausted, but were very enthusiastic about their first steps in this important part of the journey into their new professional careers. Sarah, whose food preparation skills would rival those of the best of chefs, had prepared an attractive and tasty light chicken salad dinner for them and, prior to beginning their meal, they held hands while Tim began the blessing saying, "Dear Lord, thank You for this food and for the many other wonderful gifts that You've given us; and we especially thank You for coming into Sarah's and my lives which You shall always be at the center of, and for showing us the way to happily live our personal and professional lives together. Amen."

Sarah added, "And thank you my dear Lord, Jesus for sending my dear husband home to me and for filling his heart and mind with your beautiful truths. Amen"

After they had said their prayer, Sarah then smiled and said to Tim, "I still just can't believe it, Honey, and please forgive me for bringing it up, but here we are sitting at the very same dining table where, just a few weeks ago, you vehemently denied that in which you now so strongly believe.

Remember how we had one heck of a fight over it where we both used the ugliest and meanest language imaginable toward one another? But now, thank the good Lord, you've completely changed the way you think and act about spiritual matters, and this will always be the most wonderful gift I could ever hope to receive from you and our Lord in my entire life!"

After they finished dinner, they cleaned the kitchen and said their nightly prayer; enjoyed a long, warm, and happy lovemaking session and then lovingly snuggled close together in a deep sleep.

Chapter Seven

As the weeks passed, Sarah's and Tim's internships were proving to be very challenging and, like most internships, were usually enlightening for them in most ways, and occasionally a little boring and even somewhat demeaning in others.

They usually worked different and long hours, including most weekends, and were learning a lot about medicine and life; but were sometimes required to perform menial tasks that were perceived by some of the interns as being beneath their levels of professional ability and their new status as doctors. But even these were valuable lessons in humility for them and helped them to develop an understanding of the larger life's picture beyond their M.D. status and roles.

Despite the occasional less enjoyable events, their overall experiences were very challenging and educational, especially their duties in the emergency and operating rooms where they would often be exposed to some highly dramatic life and death situations.

Late one Sunday afternoon, while Tim was assigned the duty of assisting Dr. John Hall, the head physician in the emergency room, a fifteen-year-old boy who had been badly injured when he fell from his skateboard and his legs had been run over by a car, was brought in along with his mother by an ambulance. The young boy's knees and ankles had been badly cut and broken, and he was in a great deal of physical pain.

After Tim had provided the young boy with basic life-protecting first aid and pain relief treatment under the aegis of the emergency room doctor, he was directed by Dr. Hall to keep an eye on the young boy until he could be transported upstairs into the operating room to receive some sorely needed surgery on his badly damaged legs.

With the young boy's weeping mother standing close by them, Tim knelt down beside the boy and gently held his hand while he offered a brief prayer aloud for the boy's recovery…"Dear Heavenly Father, please help this dear young boy to quickly recover from his painful injuries and please bless his loving parents with the hope and assurance that they need in this difficult time for them. Amen."

When the injured boy's mother heard Tim saying the brief prayer for her son, she became enraged and shouted, "You'd better stop that damned prayer crap right now and pay attention to my boy's health instead of saying all that stupid God talk, doctor, or I'll sue this damned hospital for everything they have!

My family and I are not religious people, and we damned sure don't want or need to hear any of that God and Jesus bull crap said by you or anyone else around my boy while he's hurting!"

When Dr. Hall heard the shouting coming from the mother in the cubicle where her son was lying in wait for transport to the operating room, he rushed in to see what was causing the ruckus.

The mother angrily and loudly said to him, "That stupid, crazy, and holy-rolling young doctor is trying to act like a damned preacher and he's been treating my boy with a lot of his crazy prayer crap instead of helping to make his hurt legs get well. I'm going to file a complaint with the hospital against that stupid excuse for a doctor if he doesn't stop it right now.

All we want is to get healing for my son and not have to listen to a bunch of damned stupid praying. If we needed that kind of bull crap, we'd have gone to one of those dumb churches instead of coming here!" Dr. Hall then called Dr. John Devore, the chief surgeon, told him what had happened, and asked how long he thought it would be before the boy could be admitted to the operating room for his needed surgery. Dr. Devore immediately came downstairs to see the young boy, and apologized to his mother for the delay in getting him into the operating room and for Tim's offensive actions.

He assured the mother that her son would be going to the operating room and be taken care of as quickly as they could get him in, and his legs should be okay after his surgery. She angrily said to him, "Okay, doctor, but y'all better keep that stupid young preaching doctor away from my boy with his holy-rolling praying crap or I'll have my husband come here and whip his young ass." Tim felt as though he had been unfairly judged and was very hurt by what he viewed as this woman's vicious and negative over reaction to his good intentions.

He thought to himself, Here I was, trying to seek God's help for the woman's son and for her, and she was acting like…he then stopped and suddenly realized…exactly like I would have probably acted just a few weeks ago! Drs. Hall and Devore pulled Tim aside and sternly advised him that he should keep his personal religious beliefs to himself and out of his medical work while he was serving as an intern.

Dr. Hall said, "If you want to quietly pray for someone, Tim, I have no problem with that; but please don't do it out loud like that anymore, because some people may not share your religious views and may even find them offensive. That's the Hospital Chaplain's job to handle, young doctor, and not yours!"

With his head hung low, Tim apologized to the doctors and said that he was only trying to help lift up the young man and his mother's spirits until he could be taken to the operating room and that he was truly sorry if he offended his mother by it. He asked Dr. Devore if he thought it would help to take some pressure off of the situation if he were to go to her now and apologize.

Dr. Devore said, "No, Tim, I don't think that would help the matter right now and it might even exacerbate her anger. I'm afraid she's still pretty upset about her son's situation and is very annoyed with you; and she might want to give you a good kick in the butt if you even come anywhere near her! I think it would be much better for you to give yourself a break, Tim, by going for a little walk in the park outside the hospital, and laying low for a while until we get him upstairs for surgery and his mother can calm down a little…but please don't do that prayer stuff out loud again, buddy, unless someone specifically asks you for it.

I know you meant well by what you did, Tim, but we have a hospital chaplain here whose job it is to provide our patients with whatever religious support they need and want. You're probably going to get your butt royally chewed out for it later by the Hospital Administrator if the woman follows through with her complaint against you, but don't let it get you down, Tim." But it did get Tim down; in fact, he found himself feeling deeply depressed and embarrassed over the situation.

As he walked alone in the park in front of the hospital, he sought the solution to his dilemma through silent prayer…"Dear Jesus, in my first direct attempt to show my faith in You to others, it seems like I really botched it up and it looks like it's going to blow up in my face if the hospital administrator hears about it. I understood that You wanted me to enlighten people who are like I once was and do not believe in you and our Father, but it seems that I must have apparently gone about it in the wrong way. How would You recommend that I handle situations like this one in the future?"

He paused, and in his mind he sensed hearing the answer clearly coming into his mind from Jesus. "Don't beat up on yourself so hard, Tim, because I know you meant well by what you did; but you should think your caring strategy through before opening your mouth the next time, and maybe express yourself a little differently, buddy. Don't you remember my telling you to walk the talk and not talk it? You should have just given the boy's mother a warm hug, and said your prayer to me for her son and her silently.

I thought I had made it clear to you that I don't need for you to be an evangelist with your mouth pal, but only in your acts. As Drs. Hall and Devore said to you, your place is as a doctor and not as a preacher, got it?" Tim then definitely got it! When his disappointing and most unpleasant first day of duty in the emergency room was finally over, Tim couldn't wait to get away from the hospital and return home.

He was clearly down in the dumps and emotionally whipped over what had happened to him in the emergency room, and had little to say. Sarah had arrived home just a few minutes before and had begun preparing their dinner. When Tim came through the door, Sarah hugged him and cheerfully asked, "Well, my beloved and handsome young doctor and husband, tell me; how did things go for you on your first day of working in the emergency room?" Tim glumly replied to her that it hadn't gone well at all. He said, "

To be honest with you, Honey, I am really kind of embarrassed over what happened to me today and would prefer to not talk about it right now if you don't mind; but I will tell you more about it later after I cool down a little." He asked how her first day of working in the obstetrics department had gone.

Sarah happily replied, "It was really a very interesting experience for me Honey; especially this morning when I participated in my first Caesarian section procedure. I must have lost ten pounds in nervous sweat when Dr. Ploeger, who's just a little older than us and is in charge of the delivery room, allowed me to assist her by making an incision on the mother's abdomen, and then suturing it closed after the baby was removed. I hadn't even sewn on a button in years, but Barbara Phillips, the P.A. who assisted her, even complimented me for my neat stitching job!

Overall, even though some of it was a little bit scary, it was a very educational and rewarding day for me. Why wasn't your duty in the emergency room a good one and what in the world happened to cause you to be feeling so far down in the dumps?"

Tim told her that he was almost ashamed to tell her about it, but would try to do it without bellyaching too much. He confessed that he had done something that was inappropriate while he was there that really made him feel like a completely dumb piece of pure crap.

He then went on to describe in detail the episode in the emergency room involving the mother and her injured son. After hearing Tim tell his story, Sarah said, "I'm so sorry for what happened to you, Honey, and I know you really meant well by what you did; but you know how some people are about religious stuff…kind of like you once were, you know. I think Drs. Hall and Devore actually gave you some pretty sound advice to follow in future situations like the one you had today." Tim told her that he agreed and that they sure did, because he really shot himself in the foot on that one, his very first big screw-up.

He added that he now realized that he had to be more careful of how he expresses himself about that kind of stuff in the future where he had gone from one extreme to another the way he had. He jokingly told her he realized that if he didn't shape up, the hospital administrator might wind up throwing his butt out of his internship and he might have to mow grass or become a male stripper for a living instead of being a physician! Sarah gave him a reassuring and sympathetic hug, and jokingly told him, "

You'd probably be a super star as a male stripper with your cool body, you sexy guy, but we both know you're gonna be an even bigger star as a doctor! By the way, Honey, while we're on the subject of your faith, when are you going to fill me in on that which you said you would when were on our way home from Savannah…about what you experienced when you were in that deep comatose state from the accident?" Tim told her that he would do that after he could calm down a little more and after they had dinner; that it would take him a while to tell her the whole story, it would probably knock her socks off, and that she may even want to have a strait jacket or butterfly net thrown over him and have him committed to the Behavioral Health Department as a complete nut case after she hears him tell her about it.

After they had finished their dinner, Sarah and Tim sat together on the living room couch and he began to share the details of all that had happened in his previous out-of-body experience with her which he could still recall in exact detail. When he was finally finished with telling her the whole story of what had happened with him, from life to death and back to life, Sarah was absolutely stunned.

"Wow, Sweetheart, what an incredibly fabulous experience you had! Do you believe it was actually for real or if perhaps your brain could have been playing tricks on you and you were hallucinating or having some kind of a delusion? Whatever it was, the experience has really changed you tremendously, Honey…and, I might add, much for the better." Tim told her that at the time all of it seemed so real to him; however, he was also beginning to wonder a little about it, himself. "Maybe it was just my injured brain playing strange tricks on me, although I hope not, because it was so seemingly real, inspiring, and enlightening to me.

Then, when I witnessed our quick recovery from our injuries and Amelia's health improvements, it further reinforced my belief that it was for real."

He added that, "Regardless of what it was, it has managed to pull my previously ignorant head out of my butt and has definitely caused me to become a true believer in God, Jesus, the soul, and Heaven; and nothing is ever going to make that go away."

They hugged and kissed; then, one thing led to another, and they soon found themselves engaged on the living room couch in a happy lovemaking session that eased his earlier feelings of stress and anxiety. Afterwards, they knelt together beside the bed, holding hands, and began their nightly prayer which ended with, "We pray the Lord our souls to take. Amen."

* * * * * *

A few weeks later, Sarah and Tim shared the same duty schedule by shadowing Dr. Cason, the Chief Psychiatrist and Director of the Behavioral Health Department…the gentleman whom they had previously met on their first day at the hospital.

Prior to beginning their rounds, Dr. Cason gave Tim and Sarah a brief orientation on the organization, mission, and procedures of the Behavioral Health Department. "Sarah and Tim, we have several types of patients here in the Behavioral Health Department, ranging from those with relatively uncomplicated and not too difficult to treat mental problems such as simple confused thinking, stress, anxiety, substance abuse, or mild depression in Wards A and B, to patients with severe and potentially dangerous psychotic conditions in Ward C, which is a secure lockdown ward.

The majority of our patients are on various psychotropic medications ranging from mild to some pretty strong ones to help keep them calm and under control until they can be treated, which is usually through intensive counseling therapy.

We are staffed with another licensed psychiatrist, two licensed clinical psychologists, three licensed clinical social workers, and four licensed professional counselors who provide the majority of the behavioral therapy for our patients. I will give you a brief background on and introduce you to each of the patients as we go through the three wards, but don't be frightened by some of the patients in Ward C, who might seem a little irrational or even hostile towards us.

We have one poor fellow in Ward C who was brought in three days ago and he's convinced that he's Jesus Christ. He becomes absolutely furious and pretty aggressive when anyone disagrees with him on what I view and diagnosed as a clearly psychotic condition." Sarah nervously asked him, "Would we be exposed to any kind of danger from being around any of the psychotic patients like him, Dr. Cason?" Dr. Cason replied, "No, Sarah, not really.

We keep any patient that we feel might become physically aggressive in the lockdown ward and in restraints to protect them as well as us. I also have two ECT procedures scheduled for later on today, which I'm sure you'll both find quite interesting to observe." Tim asked Dr. Cason if he could he tell them a little more about ECT. He said he recalled having heard a lecture about it while they were students in medical school, but they didn't go into a lot of detail about it and he hadn't actually observed one being done, so he didn't really understand it very well and would like to know more about it.

Dr. Cason replied, "Sure, Tim; electro-convulsive therapy is what was once referred to many years ago as 'shock treatment,' and it has been widely used to treat some severe types of mental disorders since way back in the early forties. I've found it to be a pretty effective means especially for treating some of the more severe cases of anxiety and depression, and even in certain types of borderline personality disorders and some psychotic behaviors.

The main problem we've sometimes experienced with it is that, although its overall effectiveness has always been pretty good, it usually leaves the patient in somewhat of a confused but more relaxed state with some recent memory loss immediately afterward that often takes the patient a good while, sometimes even several days, to fully recover from these effects.

However, it does seem to help by relieving some of their painful mental symptoms and helps to prepare them to better benefit from other forms of psychotherapy. I do admit that there's been a lot of debate about its value as a therapy by some psychiatrists, because we're not even a hundred percent sure as to exactly why it works, but my experience has shown it to generally be a good one, especially for certain types of extreme cases. If you have no further questions, let's all head out to the 'funny farm' and I'll introduce you to my 'animals'."

Tim was especially interested in meeting the psychotic patient who claimed that he was Jesus. He wondered if this poor fellow could have had an experience similar to what his had been to cause this kind of thinking, but this thought was quickly dismissed as soon as Tim met him.

The patient, a gentleman by the name of Reverend Samuel Morgan, was forty-five years old, tall, gaunt, with a heavy beard and long, frizzy hair, and held a Master's degree in Theology from Duke University. Tim immediately felt sympathetic towards him and reached over to shake Samuel's bound hand, introduced himself, and told him he was pleased to meet him. Morgan quickly pulled his bound hand back from Tim's and angrily shouted, "Damn you, you stupid sinner; don't you dare call me Reverend Morgan because that is not who I really am.

I've told all these people that I'm only occupying the body that he once lived in, and my real name is Jesus the Christ; and you doctors are going to be severely punished by my Father, God, for not believing me and for disrespecting me like this by locking me up and treating me like I'm a crazy man…you'll see!"

Sarah was taken aback and frightened by Reverend Morgan's angry and aggressive manner and clearly irrational thinking, and quickly departed from the ward.

This frightful event added reinforcement to her choice to become a pediatrician where she would work mainly with innocent and generally sweet little obedient children, and she definitely did not want to become involved in psychiatry where she would be exposed to potentially dangerous and irrational people like Reverend Morgan! Prior to meeting him, Tim had privately kept an open mind regarding

Morgan's claim because he actually had met and knew the real Jesus and had become His friend, and considered the possibility that maybe yet another strange event involving the Deity might have actually occurred in Reverend Morgan's situation.

However, Morgan's erratic behavior quickly eliminated such a thought as he was, indeed, a clearly and severely psychotic individual; but Tim still felt a special personal desire to try and help the poor man who had previously served our Lord so well in so many positive ways. When they were back in Dr. Cason's office, Cason asked Tim what his impressions were of Reverend Morgan.

Tim said that in his uneducated mind as far as he could surmise, Morgan did appear to be a pretty mentally unstable man; but that anyone who has the nerve, albeit crazy, to identify himself as Jesus will always attract his special attention and curiosity. Tim asked Dr. Cason to tell him about Reverend Morgan's background and how he happened to get that way.

Dr. Cason said, "You and I share a similar view on that topic, Tim, and I was pretty open-minded to the possibility that he had actually had some form of spiritual experience beyond my understanding when I did my initial psychiatric assessment of him. Reverend Morgan was once a well-educated AME pastor who was well liked and highly respected by his congregation and the community until one recent Sunday morning when his psyche suddenly appeared to have completely snapped.

While in the middle of delivering a stormy and passionate sermon, he suddenly spun around in a daze, and fell down on the floor…then, after a few seconds of appearing to be unconscious, he slowly stood up with raised arms and announced to the congregation that he was Jesus the Christ! His congregation was stunned by what had happened to Reverend Morgan, and many of them didn't know how to react to his announcement. Some actually believed what Morgan had said to them was so, and walked up to and bowed down to him in respect; but the majority concluded that he had simply lost it and had him brought here involuntarily.

It was a very sad situation because I understand that prior to that event he was a very highly respected husband and father of four children, and an outstanding religious leader who had just suddenly and for no discernable reason lost all contact with reality. In fact, when his caring wife of over fifteen years and their twelve year old son came here to the clinic to see him, he didn't even recognize them." Tim asked Dr. Cason how he treated a patient like that, one who is clearly delusionary and seems so far detached from reality as this poor fellow apparently was.

Cason replied, "I'll probably try electro-convulsive therapy on him and give him some time to rest; and then hope that with some good psychotropic medications and psychotherapy he will regain his once very rational and intelligent mental functioning.

Sarah, what are your thoughts about it?" Sarah replied, "I do like you very much, personally, Dr. Cason, and I certainly do have respect for your professional field; but with no offense intended, I'm becoming even more convinced from this day's experience that pediatrics will be the best path of medicine for me to pursue…and most definitely not psychiatry, because some mental illnesses seem very dangerous and difficult to diagnose and treat. Have you had any other patients who have reported that they had major spiritual type experiences?"

Dr. Cason replied, "I sure have, Sarah; quite a few of them, and one in particular which most stands out in my mind. A few years ago, I had a gentleman who had served in combat during the Viet Nam war and had been sent from the Veterans Administration to be operated on here at Cumberland County Regional for cancer in one of his lungs. His name is Chris Russell and he was a highly intelligent and likeable young fellow who had been very cooperative, polite, and rational when I first met him during the pre-operative phase of his surgery.

Later, after Chris was anesthetized and his surgery had been completed, we suddenly lost him and he couldn't be resuscitated. After he was determined to be clinically dead, his body was placed on a gurney and was waiting for about twenty minutes or so for an orderly to come and take it downstairs to the morgue. Then, all of sudden, about thirty minutes later, he sprang completely back to life and sat up!

After the surgical nurse removed the tubes from his throat and he was able to speak, Chris reported that while he was clinically dead he had actually met and spoken directly with Jesus Christ."

This really caught Tim's interest and he asked Dr. Cason if he thought this fellow, Chris Russell, might have had a real such experience or if it could have just been the result of a hallucination or some sort of a brain shutdown. Cason said, "It's really hard for me to say with absolute certainty, Tim, because nothing exactly like that one had ever happened with any of my patients before.

We have had occasional similar reports from other patients that were difficult to evaluate and assess; however, if there was ever a real one, this would have definitely been it in my opinion because, between you and me, Mr. Russell had me about convinced that it was for real, and I still feel that way."

Tim asked Dr. Cason if it would be possible for him to meet with this Russell fellow and speak with him about his experience because this issue personally interested him; but he didn't dare tell Dr. Cason why it did, least it raise Cason's doubts about Tim's own mental stability.

Dr. Cason said, "Chris's home is over in Fayetteville with his lovely wife, Susan, and both are from socially prominent Fayetteville families. He's currently temporarily working as a counselor and case manager for the Veterans Administration up in Massachusetts, but if you'd like to meet him I'll see if I can get in touch with him and ask him to contact you the next time he comes home to visit. He's a really quite a nice fellow and I know you will immediately like him as I did."

With that exciting day under their belts, Sarah and Tim departed from the hospital and headed straight for home with lots to discuss and think about… and high on Tim's list was to chat with Sarah about his newfound and growing interest about possibly doing a residency in psychiatry!

Chapter Eight

One Sunday morning when Sarah and Tim finally had their first Sunday off from several weeks of their challenging intern work and Tim's Army Reserve meetings, they were able to enjoy their first lazy sleep-in past their usual five a.m. wakeup time in months.

Sarah sat up in the bed at eight a.m. and asked Tim, "How would you like for us to stay in bed today, be lazy, and lounge around all day in our pajamas, Honey? I'm sure you could use a little extra rest after the rough last few weeks we've both had at the hospital and your Army Reserve duty.

I know I sure would like to catch up on my rest, too, because some of it has about worn me to a complete mental frazzle, especially the kind of scary psychiatric stuff we did with Dr. Cason and some of his really crazy patients!"

Tim thanked Sarah for her consideration but said he would rather get up and go to church if she didn't mind, but she was more than welcome to sleep in if she wished because she had probably experienced an even more stressful week than he.

She turned to Tim with a smile and said, "Ain't no way you're gonna go anywhere, especially to church, without me, buddy, As the Bible says in the Book of Ruth, 'Wherever thou goest, so shall I go'…or at least that's what I think it says!" Tim told her that he would feel better having her with him and that after church they could go and enjoy the great brunch they serve at the Hilltop House, the place where he first proposed to her…and then, sadly, when they both really showed their rear ends to each other by fighting like idiots after they went back to her condo.

Tim asked if she still remembered that awful nightmare of an experience. Sarah replied, "Do I remember? How can I ever forget it? Yes, I do remember it quite well, but not with any ill feelings toward you, Honey, because I really put the foul mouth on you pretty bad that night as well. I said words to you that I wasn't even sure what all of them meant, except that they were very crude and mean, and I can't apologize to you enough for losing it the way I did and by saying those awful things.

But, as we've both surely learned from that then awful experience, sometimes even terribly negative situations like that one was for us can provide the foundation for a change to a more positive one. The major changing of your views about the spiritual aspect of our lives since then has absolutely meant the world to me.

It was about the only significant difference between us then, but it was a huge one and, thanks be to God, we're now on the same page about this key part of our lives.

So, my fearless leader, let's get our best Sunday-go-to-meeting rags on and head out to church and then drive over to Fayetteville and go to the Hilltop House where we can have ourselves both some spiritual and tummy-pleasing food!" As they were about to leave their home for church, their home phone rang and Tim answered it. It was Red, his old Atheist buddy from high school.

He said, "Hey, man, where the heck have you been hiding? We haven't seen you in several months and wondered what was going on with you. Some of the guys are going to have a little get-together this afternoon at one of the new strip joints where the drinks are half-price and the gals have huge boobs, and wondered if you might be interested in joining us."

Tim politely told Red that he was sorry, but his beautiful wife and he were on their way to church to worship their Lord right then and that he no longer ascribed to their Atheistic beliefs, but he and his pals were always more than welcome to join them in church if they wished. Red immediately hung up the phone and Tim felt pretty certain that he would never hear from him and the Atheists Club guys again… and this was okay with him. Sarah and Tim then drove downtown to the church dressed up in their "Sunday best."

When Reverend Roberts saw them enter the church sanctuary, he was both pleased and concerned…extremely pleased that Tim was finally back in church again, but also somewhat concerned about his past outspoken negative attitude and criticisms toward the church, and especially how Tim had behaved at the wedding ceremony that had been conducted just a few months before.

In fact, several of the other parishioners who had also been aware of Tim's past outspoken negative and hostile criticisms of their church were also surprised and a little uncomfortable about seeing him there. When Tim genuflected towards the altar prior to entering a pew near the front of the church, then politely knelt alongside Sarah, solemnly bowed his head, clasped his hands, and began to pray, several people in the church stared at one another in utter disbelief!

In years past, when Tim had been there as a younger man, he would usually sit with his arms intentionally crossed and wear an annoyed and pouty look on his face as an act of defiance of the customary prayers offered by his family while they were on their knees praying.

These long time church members quickly noticed the large change in his demeanor and were pleased to see it! When the congregation arose and began to sing the hymn, The Church's One Foundation, Tim stood up with his hymn book in hand and sang aloud with smiling enthusiasm. Everyone noticed the major huge change in his demeanor, including the priest, who had picked up on what was happening, smiled, and nodded his approval toward Tim from the pulpit.

Tim pretty well knew what the people around him would be thinking about him and it didn't bother him one bit…in fact, it sort of pleased him, because it was his way of making a statement that he was also now a real believer and hoped it might make a positive impression on any others who might be thinking as erroneously as he once had.

This was also a reminder to him that this was the way he was supposed to accomplish the mission given him by Jesus…to walk the talk! After the service was over, Sarah and Tim joined the congregation in the parish hall for refreshments, which was a new change for him.

As a young teenage boy, he used to sit alone in his parent's car, pouting and with his arms defiantly crossed while awaiting his parent's return from the parish hall, instead of joining them and participating in the after-worship social gathering.

Then, after becoming an Atheist, he didn't even go anywhere near the church. Tim stood in the parish hall sipping on a cup of coffee and nibbling on a cookie while he chatted and socialized with some old friends, including his pleased parents, sister, and Sarah's parents.

It was an incredibly noticeable change for him, his first real participation in the social life of the church since he was around thirteen years old! Afterwards, Sarah and Tim headed for the Hilltop House for brunch where they encountered several of their other old friends, including the friendly owner and head chef, Beth, whom they hadn't seen in the months after they had their falling out, and she greeted them in her always warm and hospitable way.

They enjoyed a great brunch together and then decided to head straight to home in Dumont for the afternoon and enjoy what they had begun referring to as an "afternoon delight," which was a long, intense, happy, and very satisfying lovemaking session! It was truly a delightful Sunday afternoon for Sarah and Tim!

* * * * * *

After a restful night of sleep, both of them arose at their usual five a.m. time and prepared to head over to the hospital. Sarah was scheduled to spend some time in the operating room, and Tim was scheduled for duty in the obstetrics clinic, which made him a little uncomfortable because obstetrics was one of the fields of medicine in which he had the least amount of interest, and he kind of dreaded having to go through that required part of his practical medical education process.

He was introduced to Dr. Suzanne Ploeger, the newly assigned Director of the Obstetrics Department, who was a warm, very attractive, and friendly young lady who was only in her late twenties and the hospital's youngest department head, and she gave Tim a cordial welcoming hug.

Dr. Ploeger said to Tim, "I understand from your file that your future plans don't call for this area of medicine, Tim, but this is where all of life begins for the patients with whom you'll be working later on in their lives, regardless of your future medical specialty, and I hope you are going to find it to be an interesting, educational, and inspiring experience.

When you are in the delivery room and have the opportunity to observe an innocent and precious little baby coming out of its mother's womb to enter into this crazy world of ours, Tim, I promise that you're going to find it to be a truly awesome experience to behold." Tim then made the rounds with Dr. Ploeger, where they visited with and checked on the several about to be mothers who were in various stages of labor and awaiting the delivery of their babies.

Tim noted the sense of happy anticipation which the majority of the expecting mothers' faces reflected, in spite of the physical discomfort of labor they were experiencing. It made him think of Christmas, the day on which Jesus entered into this world in human form from the womb of his mother, Mary, and his interest in observing an actual delivery was enhanced by that positive thought.

Dr. Ploeger then said, "Okay, Tim, we're about ready to observe the miracle of a child being born in Delivery Room 2, so go and get yourself scrubbed up, and let's go and watch it happen." When Tim and Dr. Ploeger entered the delivery room, he observed an attractive young girl who was lying on the delivery table with her knees drawn up and legs spread wide apart, and she appeared to be unusually young to be having a baby.

Dr. Ploeger softly whispered to him, "Tim, our patient here, named Alice, is only thirteen years old and she is having an exceptionally tough time of it. She was walking home alone from her middle school late last year, just a couple of weeks before Christmas, when she was pulled into the woods and raped by a man she didn't know and who is now doing thirty years in prison for it.

When it became known to Alice and her parents that she had become pregnant from that horrible experience, everyone, including me, did our best to convince her and her parents that she should consider having an abortion during the early first trimester of her pregnancy. But both

Alice and her parents are very serious Christians who were strongly opposed to the idea of killing an unborn child at any stage and for any reason, and they chose to proceed with the infant's birth in spite of the unfortunate circumstances of its conception."

Tim told Dr. Ploeger that their decision sure did take a whole lot of courage on their part and he didn't know if he could do the same if she were his child, especially when you consider the possibility that the rapist could have had some really bad genetic defects to pass on to the baby. She replied, "You make an excellent point and I completely agree with you, Tim.

I even brought up that point to them in support of the option of her having an abortion in their initial counseling; but their firm answer was absolutely not. They stated that the same kind of thing could have been done to Mary, the mother of Jesus, because the people in that time and place didn't understand that she had been impregnated by the Holy Spirit and Mary had also been around this young mother's age."

Alice's contractions were now coming more quickly and painfully, so Dr. Ploeger led Tim alongside the delivery table for a close up observation of the birth. Alice puffed, panted, and strained with gritted teeth; she then gave a loud, pained scream and Tim could see the little baby's blood-covered head beginning to emerge from Alice's small body.

As the baby boy's entire body was finally completely out of young Alice's body, a wave of awe spread through his mind as he witnessed what he perceived as a beautiful and Godly produced miracle. Once the umbilical cord that connected the baby to its mother's placenta was severed and the baby let out its first cry, the newborn infant was wiped clean, tucked into a soft cotton blanket, and gently laid on his mother's breast by the nurse.

Despite the circumstances and the young mother's pain from the delivery, Alice looked down at her newborn baby son with a warm, loving, and welcome smile and gave him a soft and tender sweet kiss. Tim felt that he had just witnessed the most beautiful event of the entire human experience! When his duty day in the obstetrics ward was finally over, he profusely thanked Dr. Ploeger for allowing him to share in this wonderful and enlightening event.

He told Dr. Ploeger that actually seeing a birth happen close up had made such a deep impression on him, and he knew it would cause him to view life quite differently in the future. Although Tim admitted to her that he initially dreaded having to do this assignment, it had thus far been the most inspiring and educational experience of his medical education there, and he couldn't thank her enough for her help. Tim then went to the locker room and changed from his hospital scrubs into street clothes and headed for their home in Dumont.

When he arrived there, he couldn't wait to share with Sarah the awesome experience that he had in the obstetrics ward. But when he entered their home, he found her sitting at the dining room table with her head hung low in her hands and she was softly sobbing.

Tim sympathetically asked her what was the matter and why did she seem so upset. He assumed that something really bad might have happened to her earlier today in the operating room and asked if that was the case. "Yes it sure did, Honey," replied Sarah as she looked up at Tim through her swollen, sad, tear-filled, and reddened eyes and tightly held his hand next to her cheek. She said, "Early this afternoon, a beautiful and precious little three-year-old girl was brought into the operating room where she was suffering from a large blood loss and multiple severe wounds she had received from having been attacked and badly bitten by a vicious pack of wild dogs.

Dr. Devore, who is such a kind and caring man and a really wonderful surgeon, did everything he could to try and save the little girl, but she was too far gone and died just a few minutes after she came into the operating room.

Everyone in the room, including Dr. Devore and I, broke down in tears when it was obvious that this precious little child had not survived her ordeal. I just couldn't help myself, Honey, but when I realized that she had died, I fell to my knees and held the little girl's lifeless hand and started saying a prayer for her soul. Remembering what you told me Dr. Devore had said to you when you had your experience a few weeks ago with him in the emergency room, I was concerned that my reaction might annoy him and he would criticize me for it, but I felt that I just still had to do it, regardless of the consequences.

But do you know what Dr. Devore did? Instead of criticizing me for praying for the little girl, which I thought he would do, he knelt down on the floor beside me and put his hand on my shoulder to comfort me while I prayed. He's such a nice man and a really wonderful and caring doctor."

Tim tried to calm her and decided to postpone the sharing of his wonderful experience in the obstetrics department with her until she was more settled down from her own unhappy experience in the operating room. This just wasn't the right time for it, as Sarah's emotional comfort and peace of mind were his foremost concern.

Tim suggested that they should go get some takeout food from Taco Bell's for dinner, and then take a nice long walk afterward to help relax Sarah's very depressed state of mind.

Chapter Nine

After they had finished their light dinner of takeout tacos and Sarah had calmed down from her earlier sad and tragic operating room experience, she and Tim strolled around the neighborhood together in the twilight, holding each other's hands and discussing the interesting experiences they had thus far had as interns. They even had a few chuckles talking about some of the profoundly funny and crazy things they had witnessed and experienced.

Tim shared with Sarah that, next to the incredible epiphany experience he had while he was out of it when they were in Savannah, the past few months at the hospital had been the most enlightening experiences he ever had in his entire life, even the sad one she had experienced earlier in the day.

They agreed that this was real medicine in the real world, with more human drama, challenges, life and death situations, and surprises than they ever imagined they would experience, and not at all like the canned and planned stuff that they usually experienced while they were students in medical school. Sarah said, "Yeah, Honey, you're absolutely right…it really is the real thing.

I've also had some of the highest and lowest emotional experiences in my entire life since we've been here as well and, like you just said, they are second only to the incredible events that we experienced when we went through what we did a few months ago in Savannah." As they were walking, Tim's cell phone rang.

He answered and it was Reverend Allen Roberts, the rector of their church. "Hello, Tim, this is Allen at the church. Do you have a couple of minutes to talk with me?"

Tim told Allen that it was such a pleasure to hear from him and asked what he could do for him. Allen said, "I just wanted to tell you how good it was for me to see you and Sarah together at the church this past Sunday, and ask you how yours and Sarah's internships at the hospital were going.

Also, Tim, would it be possible for you and I to get together one day soon when it's convenient for you and have ourselves a little personal chat?" Tim told him that it was really great for him to be back in church and see him again and that it was the first Sunday they have had off of work at the hospital, along with his monthly weekend Army Reserve duty in a while, or they would have been there sooner.

Tim also told Allen that, as he probably recalled, other than at their wedding ceremony a few months ago, where he knew he really acted like a complete jerk and for which he apologized, it had been a long, long time away from the church for him personally…far too long, and that he was sure mighty glad to finally be back. He also told him that Sarah's and his internships were going very well, and that he appreciated his asking.

Allen then said, "I'm so glad to hear that things are going well for you. Tim, I'll cut to the chase on another reason why I'm calling, and share something with you that's weighing kind of heavily on my mind in a positive way. I noticed such a huge change in your church demeanor last Sunday and would like for us to have a confidential chat and ask you to share with me what's happened in your life to cause it, if you wouldn't mind.

Needless to say, it pleased me and the other folks in our church to see it all so much, and I know something pretty special has to be behind this remarkable change. Am I being too nosey or offending you by asking you to talk about this, Tim?"

Tim told Allen that it didn't bother him at all and that he would be very glad to meet with him. He told Allen that he and Sarah would be off duty again on the coming Sunday and he would get in touch with him after church and after their new weekly work schedule comes out. They could then set up a day and time for them to get together and talk about it.

Tim closed by telling Allen to give his lovely wife, Patty, their best. Afterwards, Sarah asked Tim, "What was that all about, Honey?" Tim told her that he wasn't really sure; just that their priest, Allen, was real friendly like he always is and said he said he enjoyed seeing them on Sunday.

He said Allen had asked him how the internship was going, and said he would like to meet with him because he said he noticed the huge change in him and in his attitude towards the church, and he was curious as to what brought it on. Sarah looked at Tim with a frown and said, "Honey, surely you're not going to tell him about what happened to you during your comatose epiphany experience in the Savannah hospital, are you? My gut instincts tell me that wouldn't be a very smart thing for you to do. Didn't you tell me that Jesus even advised you against doing that?"

Tim acknowledged that Jesus did tell him to be careful about discussing it with others least they think that he had gone completely nuts, so he told Sarah that he didn't plan to talk about that experience with Allen. "What do you mean you don't plan to?" Sarah asked with another frown. "But might you? I didn't think you wanted to let that information get around for fear that someone might think that you're crazy, just like Jesus told you they might."

Tim asked her if she thought he was crazy. Sarah said, "No, not at all; but you never know how other people might react in hearing such stories as yours. You'll have to admit that it's quite a bit out of the ordinary and difficult for most people to believe."

Tim told her that he would just have to play that one by ear; but that he was thinking that with his wealth of experience and Theological knowledge, Allen might be better able to understand more deeply what it was all about and may be able to provide him with some good feedback.

But Tim promised Sarah that he would be careful, though, because he sure as heck didn't want Allen to have him thrown into the nut house either! Tim told her that the only thing he would plead absolutely guilty to being crazy about is his being crazy over her...and, for that, he said, "I hope I'm never cured!" She giggled over Tim's remark and they then stood close together on the sidewalk and exchanged deep hugs and kisses beneath the setting sun.

* * * * * *

When they returned home from their walk, they saw that Tim's mother had called and left a message for him on the voice mail. Her voice sounded as though she was very upset and she asked Tim to please call her back as soon as he could.

Tim immediately returned the call and his mother answered. She spoke to Tim through choking sobs that indicated she was still clearly very upset about something.

He asked her what in the world was upsetting her so. She cleared her throat and asked, "Son, can you please come over to the house as soon as possible? I really do need to speak with you about something that's very personal and important."

Tim told her he would be there in just a few minutes. After hanging up the phone, he told Sarah that his mother said she needs to talk with him, and she seemed to be really upset about something but didn't say what it was…and she sure didn't sound at all like her usually cheerful self.

He asked Sarah if she wanted to ride over there with him while he finds out what was troubling her. Sarah replied, "No, she wants to see you, Honey. I'll be glad to go with you if you want me to, but I think it might be better for both of you if you go and see her by yourself, especially if she's as upset as you think she is. I'll come later if you feel you need me."

Tim agreed; then gave Sarah a goodbye kiss, jumped into his car, and quickly headed over to his parents' home to see what was troubling his mother. When he arrived at his parents' home a few minutes later, his mother met him at the front door and her eyes were red, filled with tears, and swollen from her obviously heavy crying.

Tim hugged her closely and asked her what had happened to upset her so badly. She sadly replied through quivering lips, "It's your father, Tim. I'm afraid that he's found someone else to be with and I think he's decided he wants to leave me for her." Tim was shocked to hear this and couldn't believe that his Dad would ever even think of leaving his mother for someone else for any reason.

Tim asked if she knew why he would do that, reminded her of how much he has always loved her, and told her that he couldn't begin to imagine his Dad even thinking about doing something as awful as that. He asked if she was really sure about that. Through sobbing tears, his Mom replied "Yes, son, I'm sad to say that I'm completely convinced of it. I had also always believed he loved me and would always be faithful to our marriage, too, as I sure have always adored him; but, like I said, it seems that he's found himself someone else that he wants to be with more than me."

Tim asked if she knew who that someone else might be. She angrily replied, "Yes, I certainly do; it's his secretary, Marilyn, the one who's worked for him in the law firm for the past five years.

Unbeknownst to me, it looks to me like they've been carrying on with a love affair for quite a long time, for at least a year that I'm pretty sure of." He asked if she was absolutely certain of that and how did she know for sure. She replied, "I went to use my computer earlier this morning but something was wrong with it and I couldn't get an internet connection, so I decided to use your father's computer while he was out taking our dog for a long walk.

He had left it signed on with his password and, without thinking, I did something I've never done before and now kind of wish I hadn't. I looked at one of his e-mail messages that had just come in earlier in the morning, and it was to him from her and it has completely broken my heart to pieces."

Tim asked her what in the world did the message say that had upset her so badly and caused her to feel he had cheated on her. She replied, "She sent him an e-mail exclaiming about the great time they had enjoyed at the legal conference they attended together in Atlanta last year, one which he told me that he had gone to by himself.

She also said that she planned to be there at this year's conference next month and couldn't wait"…she then started crying aloud and said…"to be with him again." He asked what his Dad said to her when she asked him to explain it. She angrily replied, "Of course he denied that anything ever happened between them.

He claimed that he didn't even know Marilyn would be going the first time until after he got there, and that nothing personal was going on between them…that they just shared dinner and chatted with other members of their law firm and other conference attendees."

Tim then asked his mother why she didn't believe him and what made her so sure that he and Marilyn were having a love affair. She snapped back, "Come on now, son, please be real. I didn't need photographs to convince me of what's been going on. Between his angry reactions to my looking at his email, his too strong of a denial when I questioned him about it, and when he stormed out the door and left the house, it convinced me that they are definitely involved in an affair."

Although Tim was trying to stay calm and be supportive of his mother in this time of deep sadness for her, he was also taken aback by what he had heard her say about his father whom he had always loved, admired, and respected for his consistently highly moral personal example and his faithful commitment to his mother.

Tim asked if she knew where his Dad was. She angrily snapped, "To be honest with you, Son, I don't have any idea nor do I even give a damn where he is, but I guess he's probably out somewhere with that hussy little whore of a girl friend of his, Marilyn."

Tim told her that he would see if he could reach his father and find out what was going on. He called his father's cell phone, but didn't get an answer. He then called his law office and the phone rang several times before the office voice mail came on, stating that the office was closed and directed him to leave a message.

As he was in the process of leaving a message for his father to call him back, his father's voice suddenly broke in and answered, and he was also obviously emotionally upset.

Tim asked him to stay at the office and he would be there right away so they could talk. He quickly drove to his Dad's office in downtown

Fayetteville and went into the closed law office building where he found his father sitting at his desk with swollen and teary eyes.

After giving his father a reassuring hug, Tim asked him to explain to him what had gone on between him and his mother. His father tearfully replied, "I don't really understand it myself, Son, but when I came inside our home after taking our dog for a long walk around the neighborhood a few hours ago, your mother was obviously deeply upset.

She was cold, quiet, and clearly annoyed about something, and not at all like her usually upbeat and friendly self. When I asked her to please tell me what had upset her so badly, she started screaming at me, 'You and your little whore, Marilyn, that's what's upsetting me! You can have her, John, and you can get the hell out of this house. Go on; go to her right now and don't even bother coming back because I never want to look at your cheating and lying face again'! I still wasn't sure what it was all about until I remembered getting an email earlier today from Marilyn about last year's weekend Trial Lawyer's Conference in Atlanta. As your mother didn't tell you, because she doesn't know it either since I stupidly never mentioned it, as it didn't really seem important to me.

Marilyn showed up there in Atlanta at the previous year's meeting, which came as a complete surprise to me. I later learned from one of our firm's partners, Jim Marshall, who is a widower and has been quietly dating Marilyn for a couple of years that he had invited her to go to the conference with him at the last minute. It was a personal thing between them, which didn't concern me at all.

In fact, they secretly shared with me that they were contemplating matrimony." Tim asked his father why he didn't tell her about that as it seemed to him that explaining to his mother what had actually happened would have cleared the whole thing up right away, especially the fact that Jim and Marilyn were planning on getting married.

His Dad replied, "Your mother never gave me a chance to tell her anything, son. She was the most out of control I've ever seen her, and when she made her verbal attack and accusations that I had cheated on her with my secretary and ordered me to get out of our home, I had no choice but to leave before things really got any further out of control than they already were. Believe me, it was getting real ugly, and it was definitely the worst incident we ever had in our twenty-eight years of an otherwise happy marriage together."

Through choking tears, his Dad asked, "What do you think I should do, Son? I love your mother more than I do my life; always have and always will, and I've never once even thought of cheating on her.

But I can't live like this with her unfairly accusing me of doing such a heinous thing. She's not her normally always loving self right now and, to be honest with you, I'm worried about her state of mind over this. I've never seen her act about anything as irrationally as she has over this. I just don't know what to do about it."

Tim was at a loss for words and asked to be excused while he went to the rest room. He went into a stall, closed the door, knelt, and silently prayed. "Dear friend, Jesus, You know the difficult situation I'm dealing with about my parents.

As I'm sure You can tell, I'm also very emotionally upset over it myself, and I need some guidance from You on what I should do to help fix the situation. Please help me, my Lord and best friend, because I love them both and hate to see them in such pain."

Tim paused, then sensed a voice inside his mind that said, "Get a grip on yourself first...then you should go home and explain the situation and your father's rational explanation about it to your mother in a calm manner, Tim, letting her know about the other man who had invited Marilyn to go with him and their marital intentions...then have your father come in and give her a big and reassuring hug.

It might also be a good idea to have Marilyn and Mr. Marshall, who invited her to the conference, to be available on standby, just in case they're needed to confirm your explanation."

Tim expressed his thanks to Jesus for his logical and reassuring guidance, then emerged from the rest room in a calmer and clearer frame of mind, and asked his father to come with him. Tim and his

Dad then got into Tim's car and headed toward his parents' home in Dumont.

When they were a few blocks from the home, his father said, "No, Tim, please turn around or let me out here.

I don't want to go into our home yet with the way your Mom is feeling towards me because we'll probably just get ourselves caught up into another ugly and senseless verbal battle like we just had only a few of hours ago, and that will only make this horrible situation get even worse. I'll just stay in a motel room or some other place for tonight and try to get my thoughts together; then, maybe try and deal with her tomorrow."

Tim placed his hand on his father's shoulder and told him to please just calm himself down and let him try and handle it. He told his Dad that he loved them both more than life, and he believed he had the solution to this crazy problem. He told him that while he was inside talking with her, his Dad should place a call to Mr. Marshall on his cell phone and fill him in on the situation just in case they might need for him to come over and verify what had really happened to his Mom.

When they arrived at their home, Tim told his Dad to please wait in the car while he went inside to see his Mom; then, after he could get her calmed down and speak with her, he would wave to his Dad when he should come in…and that he should be prepared to give his Mom a big hug and kiss, and assure her that he loves only her when he does.

His Dad wasn't accustomed to Tim being so assertive with him, but assured him that, although he didn't think it would do any good, he would follow Tim's directions to see what they would accomplish.

In the course of less than fifteen minutes after Tim had calmly spoken with and explained the situation to his Mom, he gave the signal for his Dad to come inside. Tim's Mom and Dad warmly greeted each other and were happily hugging and kissing each other like teenagers as she profusely expressed her apologies to his Dad for having doubted him.

Tim was pleased to no end with the results, and realized from this brief personal experience that his future calling in medicine may not be as much to deal with human skin, organs, fluids, muscles, or bones, but instead to focus on how people think, feel, and behave, and become a psychiatrist!

Chapter Ten

When Tim returned from his parents' home to their condominium, Sarah was eager to hear what had happened with his mother.

After he had shared the whole story with her, Sarah was pleased and very impressed with how well he had handled this potentially explosive matter, and had quickly brought peace back into his parents' unexpectedly turbulent state. She said, "Honey, I think this should once again be a good sign to you that psychiatry might be a highly appropriate professional calling for you to consider pursuing instead of general surgery. What are your feelings about that?"

Tim told her that she was on to something that he had also lately been giving some real serious thought to as well, and he was beginning to like the idea more each day. He then stood and firmly announced, "There will be no more indecision on that issue from this boy, Honey, because I am going to do exactly that and become a 'shrink'!"

Sarah congratulated Tim for his decisiveness with a hug. She then told him that Chris Russell, the fellow that Dr. Cason had told them about who had reported having an afterlife experience, had called while he was with his parents and left his telephone number in Massachusetts for Tim to call him back.

Tim immediately placed a return call to him. Chris was very friendly and was not only willing to meet with Tim, but seemed eager to do so and said he would be glad to fly back to Fayetteville before he ordinarily would in order for them to have a meeting. They set up an appointment to meet at Chris's home on the coming Saturday morning.

The remainder of their week at the hospital was interesting and educational, but not nearly as emotional or dramatic as the first few months had been for Tim and Sarah. Tim arose early Saturday morning in preparation for his meeting with Chris at his home.

As he was taking his shower in preparation to leave Dumont for

Fayetteville, he thought, why am I so interested in speaking with this Russell guy? Maybe we're both as nutty as fruitcakes…oh well; I'll go meet with him and see what comes out of it.

When he arrived at the Russell home in Fayetteville, Chris's wife, Susan, met Tim at the door. She was a very attractive and congenial lady who warmly welcomed him into their nicely maintained Fayetteville home. Chris came up from his downstairs den and gave Tim a warm welcoming handshake.

After having a few minutes of polite conversation with Chris and Susan, Chris said, "Please come downstairs to our den with me where we can have our chat, Dr. McDonald. Would you care for something to drink?"

Tim passed on the invitation for a drink because he didn't want another second of delay in having this talk with Chris, and followed him downstairs to his study. Once they were seated, Chris asked Tim, "What can I do for you, Dr. McDonald? My good friend, Dr. Cason, told me that you have expressed an interest in hearing about the spiritual experience I had while I was a surgical patient at the Cumberland County Regional Medical Center a few years ago.

Is that correct, Doctor?"Tim told Chris that it sure was, and to please call him Tim because he only used the doctor tag when he was working with patients; that he otherwise preferred leaving his titles at home and being just himself, especially regarding Chris's experience. Tim told Chris that he was very interested in hearing about his spiritual experience and would like to hear it directly from him rather than from a third party.

He said that he would really appreciate it if would Chris share with him in as much detail as possible what he experienced at the Cumberland County Regional Medical Center a few years ago." Chris said, "Sure, I'll be glad to. Let me give you a little background first, Doctor - I mean Tim - so you can have a better perspective on why I am so confident that what I am about to share with you actually happened to me.

I had gone through a real tough time of it many years ago when I was in the Army as an infantry first lieutenant during the war in South Viet Nam. Then the years that followed after my combat tour of duty was over and I left the Army were even tougher, mainly as the result of some pretty bad—no, stupid—personal choices I had made.

I had abused my health pretty badly from lots of heavy pot smoking, doing illegal drugs, drinking lots of alcohol, and doing a lot other stupid things that I'm now very ashamed of and no longer do. Several years later, an annual physical exam revealed that I had developed cancer in one of my lungs.

Believe me, when I was told about that, it was sure a wakeup call for me to stop abusing my body the way I had; but I hadn't given any thought at all to the even worse abuse I had been doing to my soul. My doctor scheduled me to have immediate surgery and told me it might be too late but that he would try his best to save my other lung into which, miraculously, the cancer hadn't yet metastasized. This is where the story really gets interesting, Tim.

They had me prepped for surgery and rolled me into the operating room. After I was put under with the anesthetic, I conked out, but after what seemed to be only a few minutes of being unconscious I was suddenly awake and felt myself rapidly moving away from my body and down through a fog-filled tunnel.

Then I saw a bright light at the end of the tunnel and when I got there, I had the shock of my life. You won't believe who I saw standing before me, Tim; it was Jesus! Although neither of us had physical bodies, I still immediately recognized Him. I know it may probably sound real weird to you, Tim, but I give you my word that that's really the way it was.

Jesus gave me a warm greeting and, after we had a brief conversation together, He finally told me that it wasn't my time to be there permanently yet and I had to return to life and do the things that I must do to qualify for entrance into Heaven, which He spelled out for me.

He told me that it was mainly for me to live a more honorable and morally healthier life than I had previously been living. He told me that I had to stop doing the crazy things I had been doing and begin, as He described and explained it to me, to 'walk the talk'.

After we had spoken for a while, he bade me goodbye and I then found myself again floating backwards through the fog until I realized that I was back inside my body. A short while later, after I awakened, the doctors and nurses in the operating room told me that I had actually been clinically dead for nearly an hour, and had then miraculously come back to life. I know you're probably thinking that I'm a real nut case, Tim, and I have often wondered about it, myself; but it sure seemed so real to me at the time and still does as though it had just happened. I had many other contacts with Him through prayer afterward, and still continue doing so on a regular basis. Mind you, Tim, I was never much into spiritual or religious stuff before this happened, but this experience entirely changed the way I saw myself and it made me want to live a changed life.

Like some people, I had previously viewed Jesus somewhat agnostically, if at all. But, wow! This event sure did quickly and completely change my way of thinking about Jesus and about the way I had been living my life, and He then became the center of my new chance at life that He had given me.

When I shared my story with the doctors, some believed I was suffering from some kind of a hallucination or delusion, and others seemed to think that I had made it up, but I don't think anyone really believed me except my wife, Susan, and possibly Dr. Cason. Now that you've heard my story, Tim, what are you thoughts?"

Tim told Chris that he believed every single word he had just shared with him and couldn't thank him enough for telling his fabulous and inspiring story. Tim told Chris that he hadn't told anyone else but his wife what he was about to share with him for the same reasons Chris had mentioned - for fear they would think he was some kind of a crazy nut case and have him put away in an insane asylum - but that he had a similar experience himself and it has really totally changed his life just as it had Chris's.

Tim then went on to share the details of his Heaven experience with

Chris, who did not hesitate to believe him. This serendipitous meeting with Chris was just more evidence that helped Tim to reinforce his confidence and belief that the meeting with Jesus and his deceased family members wasn't simply an hallucinatory or delusionary experience, but it had actually happened to him.

He was also reminded of Jesus' words to him regarding what he was to do with his life as being exactly the same ones as Chris had received from Him…to walk the talk! When Tim returned home, he shared what he had learned from his meeting with Chris with Sarah and she was both amazed and pleased to hear of it, as it also helped to reinforce her belief that Tim's experience wasn't an imaginary experience at all, either, but was definitely for real.

* * * * * *

The next day, Sarah and Tim again attended church together and were met with smiling faces from those who had been somewhat surprised by their entrance into the church on their previous visit. They felt comfortable with the congregation and were pleased to see Susan and Chris Russell there, and were happily surprised to even see Dr. Devore and his lovely wife, Diana, there as well!

Their presence was reassuring and much appreciated by Sarah and Tim! During the worship service, Tim felt an impulse to turn around and look behind him.

He experienced a really huge surprise when, of all people, his buddy, Jerry Hart, the red-headed leader of his old high school Atheist group, and two of the other group members and their wives had quietly slipped into the pew behind them and gave Tim a smiling thumbs up!

Tim could hear Jesus' voice saying to him, "Atta boy, Tim…you nailed some big ones for the team…great fishing, good buddy!" Afterwards, Tim and Sarah attended the coffee and refreshment social gathering in the parish hall when, to Tim's delight, Jerry and his friends walked up to him and expressed their thanks to him for causing them to want to give God another try.

Red and some of his ex-Atheist friends, along with their wives, would later become very active members of the church! The Rector, Allen Roberts, then walked up and gave Sarah and Tim a welcoming hug.

While Sarah was chatting with one of her friends, Allen pulled Tim aside and asked if there was a chance that the two of them could get together for a short while later on that day for the chat that he had mentioned to Tim awhile back?

Tim told him he would be glad to…just tell him where and when he would like to meet." Allen asked, "Would this afternoon in my church office work for you?" Tim told him that was fine and asked him what time was best for him." Allen replied, "Right after lunch would be great for me if it works for you, Tim. Would around two o'clock be okay with you?"

Tim told Allen that it sure would; that he would definitely be there and was looking forward to it. At exactly two o'clock that afternoon, Tim arrived at the church office where Allen greeted him. They poured themselves a glass of iced tea and then went upstairs to Allen's office for their talk.

After they sat down, Tim asked Allen what was on his mind. Allen replied, "Tim, I have a strong gut sensing that something very special has recently happened in your life that has significantly changed your views towards our church; and, believe me, my friend, nothing could have been more pleasing to me.

Being the curious guy that I am, though, I've been wondering if you might be willing to share with me what might have caused this big of a change in you. I know I'm sometimes too much of a 'why guy,' and my dear wife, Patty, will sure attest to that, and I hope I'm not being too nosey or offending you by asking you about this, but it has really caught my deep interest."

Tim said that it was not a problem at all; that he appreciated Allen's interest and would be very glad to share it with him; but asked if he would please promise that he would keep it between them because after he hears his story, if he lets it out others may think that he's some kind of a nut case…which he conceded that he might well be. Allen said, "Hey, buddy, there's a little bit of insanity in all of us, including yours truly, to which I'm sure my dear wife, Patty, will also probably quickly attest.

But when whatever it was that affects people as positively as it has obviously affected one as bright, although very negative towards the church, as you once were, it deserves a different label than insanity… perhaps a miracle would be a more appropriate word to describe it!"

Tim said that was an excellent and very appropriate label for some things that have recently happened in his life, because they were all indeed nothing short of a real miracle…a huge one!

Tim went on to tell Allen that he had probably no doubt known from talking with his parents and observing his pretty negative and inappropriate behavior over the past few years as far as the church goes, he had reached not only an atheistic view and pretty negative attitude towards what the church teaches and is all about, but had also even become pretty hostile towards it.

Then something very huge had recently happened in his life that suddenly completely changed all of his thinking about a lot of things and especially the church, God, Jesus, Heaven, our souls, and you name it. "And what might that something have been, Tim?"

Allen asked. Tim paused for a few moments and then told Alan that he may not believe him when he tells him what he was about to, and he may think him to be completely nuts, but he had personally met and spoken with our Lord and Savior, Jesus Christ. But Allen didn't appear to be as shocked at hearing this statement as Tim had expected he might be.

Tim asked him if what he just said seemed strange and a kind of shock to him. Allen replied, "No, Tim, it doesn't surprise me at all. In fact, I've also met Him; perhaps not in the same manner as you may have, which I hope you'll share with me, but the beautiful logic of His life and teachings connected solidly in my mind and made a lasting intellectual and deeply spiritual impression on me earlier in my life when my beliefs needed to be supported with something more substantive than just a lot of nice sounding holy words, pretty music, stained glass windows, fancy duds, and an attractive church building.

Making that connection with Jesus as my wise and most caring friend and His guiding force deep inside my psyche is pretty much what motivated me to go into the ministry career that I chose, and not just because several other members of my family, including my own father, had done before me. I then felt that I really knew Jesus; and not just from a deep theological perspective, but also from a strong intellectual and personal one. Enough about me; so how about telling me about how you met our Lord, Jesus, in person, Tim?"

Tim told Allen that he had better fasten his seat belt for this one, because even he still found it hard to believe that it really happened to him.

He told Allen that he had actually met Jesus face-to-face; or a more appropriate way to describe it would be that, they had met soul to soul, and had a lengthy conversation together in Heaven, just like he and Allen were having, and they discussed a lot of very important things. "You met Jesus soul to soul and in Heaven? Please explain what you mean by that, Tim,"

Allen asked. Tim then went on to describe his experience with Jesus in Heaven in detail, all the while wondering what Allen might be thinking. When he was finished telling his story, Tim asked Allen what he thought and if he believed the story. Allen said, "Tim, as you may have often heard, 'With God, all things are possible'. Do I believe you? Why shouldn't I? In fact, I actually envy you for what happened to you and your good fortune of actually being in the presence of our Lord, Jesus, and I deeply appreciate your courage in sharing it with me.

Frankly, while I am truly enjoying my present Earthly life and my role in it, I'm actually looking forward to the great day when I will also be able to fully experience what you've apparently had an excellent preview of." Tim asked Allen if he thought he was a complete nut case. He replied, "No, Tim, I absolutely do not.

Too many people are closed off to having any experiences that are outside the normal boundaries of their everyday lives that they can't explain, but you sure aren't crazy in my opinion and, again, I really do appreciate your willingness to share your wonderful experience with me.

Wow! You're a mighty lucky guy, my friend." After a few more minutes of chatting, Allen and Tim shared handshakes and hugs; then Tim departed from the church and headed for home.

* * * * * *

When he returned home, Sarah was very eager to find out how the meeting with Allen had gone. She asked, "Did you actually share the whole story about your experience in Savannah with Allen, Honey?

Now please be honest about it with me and tell me the truth." Somewhat embarrassingly, Tim replied to her that he had told Allen everything…that he hadn't really planned to do it at first; but once he and Allen started chatting, he just couldn't help himself and had to let it all out. "And what was his reaction to it, Honey? Do you think he really believed you?" Sarah asked.

Tim told her that he felt pretty sure he did; at least he didn't call 911 and have him locked up! He added that he seriously found Allen's reaction to be highly reassuring and it, along with Chris's story, had helped to further reinforce his belief that it did actually happen the way he remembered it, and it wasn't some kind of an hallucinatory or delusional experience as he was beginning to fear it might have been after spending some time with Dr. Cason and Reverend Morgan while they were doing their tour on the psychiatric ward. Sarah said, "I have an idea, Honey; let's give our minds a little break from all this heavy, mind-boggling and deep stuff that we've been dealing with lately and have ourselves some plain old fun. Since we have this coming Monday off from the hospital, how about you and I driving down to Carolina Beach and going for a spin out in the ocean in your father's old friend, Ed's, old boat?

He told us that we'd be welcome to use it any time we wanted and I think it would be really good fun for us to go for a cruise out into the ocean, chill out, and enjoy a little change of pace and scenery. Since we've never tried it, I have a silly fantasy in my naughty little mind that we might enjoy having a little outdoor love making in the sunshine, something we've never done before, when we're a few miles out from shore. Are you game for participating in that 'sorta naughty little fantasy of mine, my dear husband, best friend, and lover?"

Tim gave her a wide smile and asked what did she think…like how could he possibly turn down such a cool invitation as that? He agreed that it sounded like fun and that he would love to go on out there and get it on with his beautiful, adorable, and wonderful sexy wife!

After a two hour drive, Sarah and Tim pulled into the parking lot of the beach home owned by Tim's uncle and aunt, Mal and Janie King, at a place called "Captain's Quarters," a luxurious Carolina Beach condominium complex, and headed straight for their friend's thirty-five-year-old boat, the Options II.

After loading their gear aboard it, they cranked up the two engines, untied the ropes, and headed north up the inter-coastal waterway and then turned east and out into the beautiful Atlantic Ocean.

It was a bright, sunny, and clear afternoon with a generally calm and slightly rippling ocean which was reflecting the afternoon sun like millions of tiny sparkling diamonds as they headed to a spot about ten miles out from the shore.

They then dropped the boat's anchor and both of them removed all their clothing in order to catch some tanning sunrays before the sun began to set. They played CDs of their favorite pieces of music, including Sarah's favorite, Beethoven's Moonlight Sonata, and Tim's favorite of Verdi's operas, LaTraviata.

Then, after sharing an intensely exciting and enjoyable lovemaking session on the outer deck under the sun, they stretched out on the boat's bow, feeling very relaxed and very, very happy. Sarah said, "I know your trip to Heaven was a beautiful experience for you, Honey, but I've not been there yet; so what we're sharing together way out here on the ocean is probably the closest I'll ever get to it while I'm alive here on Earth, and it sure was purely heavenly to me!"

Tim told her that, for him, the joys of being here in this beautiful setting and physically expressing their wonderful love for each other did come pretty close to being there for him, too. He said that every cell in his body was contented and at peace, thanks to God and his wonderful wife. Sarah added, "Of all the many beautiful gifts that our wonderful God has given us, sharing our deep love for each other like we just did was up there right at the top of the list of our many blessings!"

They then put their clothes back on, pulled up the anchor, and let the boat drift for a while, as they listened to more good music, caught a few more sun rays, and relaxed before they cranked up the engines and headed back to shore.

After refueling and docking the boat, before going back home they decided to enjoy a super seafood dinner, including Sarah's favorite seafood of soft-shelled crabs at the Pirates' Cove restaurant.

Chapter Eleven

Early the next morning, Sarah and Tim crawled out of their bed at the usual five a.m. time and prepared to go to the hospital and begin the eighth month of their internships. Tim was scheduled for a tour of duty in the Geriatric Nursing Facility and Sarah would be working with cancer patients on the Oncology Ward.

Tim had thought to himself that he really wasn't very excited about working with a lot of very old folks but, then again, he recalled having had the same attitude about his tour in obstetrics with the mommies and their babies, and that proved to be an amazing and very positive experience for him, so he decided to give this one his best shot.

In his mind, he could hear his Heavenly mentor, Jesus, saying to him, "You should never assume anything that you must do in your training to be good or bad before you actually give it a try, Tim, but only judge it after it's over rather than before it begins and you'll get a lot more out of it," and this made good sense to Tim, based on his thus far internship experiences. He met with Dr. Joe Alexander, who served as the director of the geriatric inpatient assisted living program, and he couldn't have been more friendly or hospitable to Tim.

In fact, early in their initial conversation, Dr. Alexander had asked Tim to address him as Joe, and not as Dr. Alexander, and Joe revealed that he, too, was not as pompous or arrogant about his title as some of his other colleagues were often prone to be, and was also a strongly committed Pentecostal Christian.

Dr. Alexander, who had been practicing various aspects of medicine for around forty years, said to Tim, "What you're going to experience here, Tim, is working with elderly patients who are in the late fourth quarter or ninth inning of their lives, and most of them are very aware that their Earthly lives are approaching the end…and many are already focusing their thinking beyond the grave and on the hereafter.

Some of the patients may seem a little strange to you at first, Tim, especially those who are suffering from the many types of disorders frequently experienced by the elderly such as a severe loss of hearing, joint pains, difficulty in walking, mental depression and various forms of dementia like Alzheimer's; while many others will amaze you with their depth of wisdom, experience, and unusually positive attitudes toward life...and even towards their forthcoming mortal death for many of them.

If you will always keep an open mind to what these older folks have to share with you, Tim, I believe you will find geriatrics to be a quite interesting and enlightening area of medicine for you to understand just as it has been for me." Dr. Alexander and Tim then toured the assisted living and nursing facility together, which was located in a separate building apart from the main hospital.

It was very nicely appointed and had a large dining room, a room for card playing, a visiting room, a light exercising gym, a large screen television set, a small library, and attractive, individually decorated private bedrooms.

Dr. Alexander then took Tim on the rounds and introduced him to several of his patients, many of whom were very hard of hearing, experiencing visual loss, and were either wheelchair-bound or required to use walkers.

The first patient Tim spoke with was a tall, balding, and grey-haired old gentleman in his middle nineties who was a retired Army Colonel and somewhat resembled how Tim recalled his deceased grandfather as looking during his final Earthly days. Colonel Edwin Watkins was a West Point graduate who also held a Master of Business Administration degree from the University of South Carolina and had served in the Second World War, the Korean, and Viet Nam wars as an infantry officer and had received numerous awards for his gallantry and service, just as Tim's grandfather had.

The old Colonel's health had recently been somewhat declining, and he had become weak and barely able to stand or walk without assistance. Tim introduced himself to the old gentleman who, although he spoke in a weakened voice, was very charming and lucid, and he seemed glad to speak with Tim. "It's always such a pleasure for me to meet and speak with you young fellows who are just beginning your long and interesting journey down the road of life, Doctor.

I've sure enjoyed my long trip, and I don't think I'd change a single thing that I've experienced in my life, even if I could…both the good and the bad," the old man said to Tim with a warm smile.

Tim told Colonel Watkins that it was a really special honor to meet him as well. He said he felt fortunate in being able to be of help to the fine folks who have lived so much more of life than he, and saluted him for his many years of service to our country. He asked the old man to please let him know if he could be of help to him in any way, asked how he was feeling, and if there was anything that he needed today.

The old Colonel replied with a smiling chuckle, "I'm feeling just fine, thank you, Doctor, but I could use a hot, young thirty-year-old chickadee to warm my bed at night if you can get me one, although I'd be like a dog chasing a bus… wouldn't know what to do with it if I caught it, and would have a helluva hard time explaining it to my dear wife, Elizabeth, when I get to see her again soon; so, on second thought, Doc, I'd best cancel that order!"

They both chuckled and Tim appreciated the old gentleman's risqué sense of humor. Tim then proceeded to take his vital signs, which he found to be in fairly decent condition for his advanced age.

Tim asked the Colonel how it was to have served in three pretty harrowing wars in which he had been an airborne infantry officer in the Second World War and Korean War, where he commanded units from platoons through a battalion, and finally served as an infantry brigade commander during the war in South Viet Nam.

The old Colonel said, "I wouldn't be honest if I didn't tell you that a lot of it scared the pure crap out of me at the time, Doctor, but the good Lord protected me and I'm mighty grateful to Him for that. I expect that I'll be seeing Him pretty soon, face-to-face, and I look forward to personally thanking Him for protecting my then 'kinda wild and crazy young butt."

Tim asked the old fellow if he had any hobbies or special interests. The Colonel replied, "I guess my only real hobbies now at my ancient age are mainly in snoozing and recalling the many past happy events from the wonderful life I've been blessed with and reliving some of them in my mind.

One of my favorite things that I still enjoy doing is watching my old alma mater, the University of South Carolina Gamecocks, where I earned my Master's degree, play football; especially when they whip the crap out of those damned old Clemson Tigers, and I especially enjoy recalling and reliving in my mind the many wonderful times that my dear wife, Elizabeth, and I shared together while she was alive and here on Earth with me. She passed away earlier this year, and I get really excited when I think about being able to see her beautiful face again one of these days real soon.

Elizabeth was my very best friend in the world and the most wonderful wife any man could ever ask for. She was always such a socially-minded gal who's probably been having herself a ball up there in Heaven while she's waiting for me to show up.

That sweet little gal of mine always had the best attitude toward life of anyone I've ever known, and she left this world with the happiest smile on her beautiful face because she knew for sure where she was going."

It was so touching for Tim to hear the old fellow's confidence about going to Heaven and his love for his wife of over seventy years. It was quite apparent that the Colonel was a true believer, and Tim asked if he had always been that way. The old Colonel replied, "No, Doc, I'm ashamed to tell you that I sure haven't. In fact, earlier in my life I guess I was somewhat of an agnostic, and didn't give a damn about much of anything, especially anything having to do with religion; but I had an experience several years ago while I was in Viet Nam that helped bring me to my spiritual senses.

Did you ever hear about the 1968 Tet Offensive in South Viet Nam? Probably not, since you're such a young pup compared with me. Well, the North Vietnamese Army had overrun many of the American and

South Vietnamese units, including mine, and we had suffered a lot of casualties.

Many of the soldiers in my unit were killed or wounded during the battle, and I was hit in the middle of my back by a large chunk of shrapnel from the enemy's mortar fire. I was having terrible pain like you couldn't imagine, could barely move, and I assumed that I was about to die at any minute. I then started praying.

You're gonna think I'm a real nut case when I tell you this, Doc, but as I was lying there on the ground, soaked in blood, hurting something awful, and expecting to die at any second, I swear to you that I heard what I believe was the voice of Jesus speaking to me.

He said, 'Don't you worry, Edwin, and just hang in there, pal, because you're going to make it'…and I damned sure did, thanks be to our wonderful God!" Tears began to well up in the old Colonel's eyes and Tim gave him a warm hug of empathic understanding. Tim then saw a lovely and smiling elderly black lady sitting alone in the library and reading a book. He introduced himself to her and she welcomed the opportunity of chatting with Tim. Unlike most of the other elderly people in the facility, she rose effortlessly from her chair, shook his hand, and said, "Hi, Doctor; I'm pleased to meet you.

My name is Margaret and my friends call me Margie. I just turned one hundred and three years old a week ago, and I'm almost embarrassed to tell you that I still feel fantastic! Most of my friends here have joint pains, trouble walking, hearing, and seeing; and many of them can't even think clearly. It really makes me wonder why I've been so lucky by being left out of having those kinds of things that old folks are supposed to experience, like knee and hip replacements, hearing aids, and all of that other old folks stuff!

Maybe I should complain to the hospital for leaving me out of those experiences," she said with a sweet chuckle.

Tim told her that she was an absolutely amazing lady and should feel especially blessed to be in such great mental and physical shape at her age. "I do feel so blessed, Doctor, and know that a lot of even greater things are awaiting me when I pass on to the next life, which I realize could happen at any moment, given my age. I'm looking forward to the wonderful experience of seeing Willis, my dear husband of seventy-four years, again and many of my old friends…and, most of all, I'm looking forward to meeting our dear Lord Jesus Christ in person!" Margaret and Tim enjoyed a nice long chat for a long while, and he was amazed at her sharp intellect, great physical condition, bright sense of humor, and confidence in the Heaven that was awaiting her.

After enjoying their chat, Tim finally left to visit with some of the other patients. On the following day, he would learn that Margie had quietly passed on to the next life in her sleep that night, and did so with the deepest smile on her beautiful face.

He chatted with several of the other elderly patients during the remainder of the day which was also very touching, interesting and educational and, in some ways, even more enlightening than his tour in the obstetrics ward had been… and it helped him to develop a better appreciation for both ends of the spectrum of life!

He then thanked Dr. Alexander–Joe–for the enlightening experience and headed back home.

* * * * * *

Sarah shared with Tim that her tour of duty in the Oncology Unit wasn't nearly as depressing as she had feared it might be, either; especially when she knew she would be seeing some of the young children who were there, with most of them on the verge of certain death from various forms and final stages of cancer.

She said that most of the patients were from many age groups and were in pretty rough physical shape; yet most of them appeared to have accepted their fate, and many had even managed to develop a sense of humor about their mostly near terminal medical conditions.

Sarah told of one perky and very upbeat lady in her mid-fifties, Helen, who had laughingly said to her, "Thank goodness for the chemotherapy that got rid of all my hair, Doctor, because I've already saved several hundred dollars from what I used to pay in weekly hairdresser fees to keep it looking good, and now they'll only have to put a cheap fifty dollar wig on my bald head for the showing of my radiation burned-out old carcass when I'm put on display in a fancy box down at the funeral parlor!"

She laughingly added, "I hope my poor husband, Bill, won't be embarrassed at how awful my once pretty cool body will look, laying there in that fancy and expensive coffin; but if he is, that's just tough, because I'll be having myself a good old time up there with Jesus in Heaven!"

Sarah then told of meeting a small ten-year-old boy, Bobby, whose cancer had metastasized throughout his frail little body and, although the young fellow knew he was close to dying, he smilingly told Sarah that he hoped Jesus would find him some new video games to play with and keep him posted on all of the baseball and football scores after he dies and goes to Heaven! Sarah asked Bobby which video games he liked best but didn't have, and she made a list to pick up some for him at Wal-Mart.

The bottom line for the day with Sarah and Tim was that they had both developed a deeper appreciation for life and were impressed with how so many of these people who had so little of their Earthly lives left were showing such brave spirits and confidence that they would soon be with Jesus in Heaven!

Chapter Twelve

That evening, after they had returned home, Tim's mother called Sarah and said she had some wonderful news to share with them about Amelia. She reported that Amelia's neurosurgeon had just examined her and reported that the previously dead and severed nerves in the lower part of her body appeared to have somehow become reconnected and seemed to be coming back to life, and she was rapidly gaining feeling in and control of her legs.

Dr. Jaufman told her there were no discernable medical explanations for what had happened to her, and he predicted that with just a little more improvement and a few more weeks of physical therapy there was a good chance that she might become able to walk normally again!

Upon sharing the good news with Tim, Sarah said to him, "This is yet another confirmation that what you thought you had experienced in Heaven really happened, isn't it, Honey? Let's kneel together and thank God for this incredibly wonderful blessing." They did, and then immediately drove over to Tim's parents' home to see Amelia.

Amelia, who had just turned twenty-one years old and was in her senior year as a Chemistry major at Methodist University, had just returned from her therapy session at the neurology clinic, and couldn't wait to show off her new abilities for Sarah and Tim.

She slowly raised herself out of her wheelchair, began walking with crutches and was actually moving her legs for the first time since she was five years old, and was no longer wearing those thick eyeglasses!

She was initially a little wobbly and unsure of herself, but once she became steadied; she began proudly prancing around on the crutches, and happily exclaimed, "My prayers are being answered!" Tim smiled, knowing that it was just a matter of a little more time before Amelia would be fully recovered and may be even able to run for the first time in sixteen years! Tim knew it because Jesus had promised him that it would happen!

* * * * * *

A few more months passed without any major problems until Tim and Sarah soon found themselves entering into the final phase of their internships. Sarah had committed herself to a career specialty in pediatrics and had been accepted by the Cumberland County Regional Medical Center to do her residency there, even though she had received offers from other larger and better known specialty children's hospitals.

Tim had been contacted by the commander of a local US Army Reserve Medical unit and was offered a promotion to Captain and a transfer to the Army's Medical Corps upon completion of his internship. Sarah and Tim discussed it at length and decided it would be an appropriate thing for him to do; especially since his father, grandfather, and great-grandfather had all served in the military.

Another advantage that it could offer was that he could do his residency in the military, probably at nearby Fort Bragg, and the Captain's pay rate would offer them better money and more benefits than most civilian hospitals would.

Tim accepted the Army's offer and was scheduled to report to the Army Medical Center at Fort Sam Houston in San Antonio, Texas after his basic internship was completed for three months of Basic Army Medical Officer Training.

Also, primarily to please his father and honor his grandfather who had both served in the 101st Airborne Division, he volunteered to attend the three weeks of basic airborne training (jump school) at Fort Benning, Georgia.

* * * * * *

Early one morning as Sarah and Tim were getting ready to leave their home for the hospital, Sarah suddenly ran into the bathroom and began to vomit.

When Tim heard her gagging and coughing, he rushed in to see what was wrong. After her stomach had expelled its yucky contents into the toilet, Sarah flushed it, wiped her face, refreshed her makeup, and then appeared to be okay.

She told Tim that she had been experiencing mild nausea like that nearly every morning for the past few days.

He suggested that she get herself a checkup from the staff gastroenterologist while she was at work to see what could be causing her stomach to feel so uncomfortable and queasy, and have him prescribe an appropriate medication for her.

The two of them went through their duties that day, with Tim spending more time making psychiatric rounds with Dr. Cason and Sarah with Dr. Finch in pediatrics. Sarah was the first to be dismissed and allowed to go home for the day, and Tim followed her shortly afterwards.

When he entered their home, Sarah greeted Tim with a wide smile on her beautiful face and said, "Welcome home, my precious young Daddy."

He asked her with a puzzled look why she was calling him daddy. He said, "I'm not your daddy am I? I always thought I was just your husband!" Sarah hugged him and laughingly said, "No, Honey, you're not my daddy, but you're the daddy of our baby that's growing inside of my belly and will be with us in about eight months!"

Tim and Sarah hugged, and they happily danced around the room together, shouting over and over, "We're gonna have a baby…hooray!" The main topic for both Sarah's and Tim's families suddenly became their forthcoming blessed event.

To its owner, Michael Fleischman's delight, both families had nearly bought out Fleischmann's Tiny Town, the popular Fayetteville children's store, of all their baby supplies.

When Sarah's obstetrician later determined their baby's gender, there was much more rejoicing in the families and even more buying of baby things for him because it was exactly the gender they wanted their first child to be… a boy!

Even though Sarah was in the advanced stage of her pregnancy, she continued in her duties as a resident in pediatrics while Tim was away for his training at the Fort Sam Houston Army Medical Center in San Antonio, Texas; but he managed to fly home on alternate weekends. Sarah would fly to San Antonio on some of the other weekends, so things were working well for them.

* * * * * *

One evening while Tim was taking an evening walk alone in downtown San Antonio near the beautiful and famous River Walk, he was approached by a disheveled Mexican man who claimed that he had a gun in his pocket and demanded that Tim give him his wallet or he would have to shoot him.

The man tearfully and apologetically told Tim that his family was starving and that he was sorry to have to rob him but he had no other choice.

Tim surprised the pathetic man when he told him that he didn't have very much cash on him, but he would be glad to go to an ATM and get some more money for him and his family. Surprised at Tim's willingness to help him, the man followed Tim to the nearest ATM where Tim withdrew two hundred dollars in cash and handed it to him.

The Mexican man was so grateful to Tim for doing this, apologized for his desperate action, and handed his pistol over to Tim, which Tim then dropped into the river. After the man departed, Tim could hear in his mind an "atta boy" coming straight from Jesus for his act of unselfish caring.

* * * * * *

Sarah and Tim were able to purchase a new home in a charming small subdivision, which was less than a mile away from the Cumberland

County Regional Medical Center.

They immediately began spending much of their spare time and lots of money in decorating and furnishing the nursery in their new home, which would soon be occupied by their little son whom they had already named Timothy Dickson McDonald, Jr.!

Sarah was in the final week of her residency and had just successfully completed her board certification examination when on a late Friday evening after she had picked Tim up at the Fayetteville airport, she suddenly began experiencing labor pains, and he rushed her over to the hospital where Dr. Ploeger and her P.A., Barbara Phillips, were waiting for them.

After spending less than two hours in labor, Sarah delivered the little fellow with relatively little pain and with Tim proudly and happily standing beside the delivery table.

He saw his little son make his initial entrance into the world weighing eight pounds and eight ounces, and he was in perfect health! At about the same time Sarah was about to become a board certified pediatrician, she also became a very happy and proud baby certified mommy! Tim, Junior, whom they lovingly nicknamed "TJ," instantly became the leading celebrity in the McDonald and Townsend families, and he was as perfect a little baby as one could ask for.

Both Sarah's and Tim's proud parents adored their little grandson, and would seize every opportunity they could to keep him at any time while Sarah was occupied with work, sometimes to the point of even arguing about whose turn it was to take care of the cute little fellow! Tim was also a week away from completing his training at Fort Sam Houston and was scheduled to begin airborne training afterwards.

After finishing jump school, he was assigned to the 82nd Airborne Division and was able to work out an arrangement with the Army to complete his residency in psychiatry at Fort Bragg's Womack Army Medical Center, which was only a twenty minute drive from their home, while he was also serving as a Brigade Medical Officer.

Sarah accepted an offer from Dr. Finch to work at his very nice pediatric clinic, which was conveniently located only a few blocks from their home.

Their plan was for Sarah to work in Dr. Finch's clinic for about a year and then consider opening her own individual practice after she had acquired some clinical management experience.

* * * * * *

When little TJ was two months old, Sarah and Tim decided that it was time to have the little fellow baptized. Tim called the church to schedule the important event. Reverend Roberts was delighted to hear this and said to Tim, "I'm mighty happy for you good folks and I look forward to baptizing little TJ. You people are such good friends and have become special assets to our church family.

When your busy schedules will allow you to we'd sure like to see if you might be interested in getting involved in one of our several church projects. I know you're both probably terribly busy with your new professional work and taking care of little TJ, but we'd sure love to have you consider giving the church a little bit of your time by advising us in the development of a plan for setting up a medical clinic at our mission for disadvantaged people in the Central America country of Belize who have no means of getting decent health care." Allen showed Tim photographs of the mission and provided him with details about the country, culture, etc. and it was obvious that Tim was becoming very interested in getting involved.

Tim told Allen that it was an interesting possibility to him, and he would discuss it with Sarah that evening, hear her thoughts, and would get back to him soon and let him know.

* * * * * *

That evening at dinner, Tim shared the conversation about the mission in Belize that he had with Allen earlier in the day. He told her that Allen had told him about a mission in a very poor part of the country of Belize which the church is supporting and where they could help them in setting up a health clinic and visiting it about once a year with their skills, and maybe even recruit some of their other medical colleagues to pitch in and help out as well.

After listening to him, Sarah replied, "Honey, I'd love to help out and get more involved in some things to help support the church, but I don't know how in the world we could find the time for it or what we might be able to do in helping them with their work.

Between spending an average of ten hours a day at the clinic and taking care of our son, I don't know how we could possibly squeeze any more activities in to our busy schedules."

Sarah added that she didn't think she had even heard of Belize before, and asked Tim where it was located and what he knew about it.

Tim told her that it was a relatively small, and pretty economically poor but very beautiful English-speaking country located on the Caribbean Sea in Central America, just south of Mexico, east of Guatemala, and north of Honduras, and the church's mission that's located there needs a medical doctor to visit for a week or two each year to help some of the people there who were in pretty rough physical shape.

He also told her that Allen had told him he was thinking about starting up a clinic to be sponsored by the church for indigent people living near the mission, which is located in one of the poorest areas of Belize; and the people there desperately need the kind of help that they could provide for them." Sarah asked him, "Have you gone totally insane, Honey?

How in the world could you and I possibly find two weeks a year to spend anywhere with all that we're having to do now between our Board certification preparations and taking care of TJ?

And you don't even know if you could get any leave time from the Army to get involved with something like that."

Tim told her that he understood her point of view but there was something inside him that made him want to give less fortunate folks elsewhere the kind of help they need and which he and Sarah would be able to give them.

He also told her that while they were certainly not wealthy, at least not yet, they had been pretty well blessed, financially, and should have a pretty hefty six-figure income coming in within the next six to eight months between them.

He said that he felt that they should give some of what they had been blessed with to others who are in need of help. Sarah told him she completely agreed with him that they should do more for the church, but asked why could they not just give a larger financial pledge amount or something like that to the church, so as not to drain them of the precious little time they have together as a family.

Tim told her that he definitely did intend for them to increase their financial pledge to the church as soon as their incomes would allow them to, but that he would also like to give some of themselves as well.

In addition to their helping others who are less fortunate, he thought it would be kind of neat for them to spend some time in that part of the world once a year…sort of like a working vacation away from their daily routines here…a different kind of life. Sarah asked Tim with a winced face, "Okay, 'Mister Save the World', suppose we should decide to give the Belize thing a shot; then what would we do with TJ? Have you forgotten that we have a little son?

We couldn't expect our parents to take care of him for that long, and I don't think I would be happy being away from him for that much time either." Tim asked Sarah why they couldn't just take him along with them. Frustrated, Sarah threw up her hands and sarcastically said, "Have you gone totally nuts, Honey?

He's barely a year old and has just started walking. I don't think he would do well being with us living out in the middle of a jungle somewhere. What would we live in; a thatched hut, tent, or something like that, with no plumbing, no electricity, or anything like what we're used to having? Or would we just live in a tree and play like we're Tarzan, Jane, and Boy by swinging on vines and living on bananas and coconuts?"

Tim told her that he understood her concerns about it, but he didn't think it would really be nearly as bad as she thought. He told her that

Allen had some videos that had been taken of the village where the church's mission is and suggested that they borrow them from him and take a look at them together to see if it might be of interest to them.

Sarah agreed that she would reserve her final judgment on what she viewed as a completely unworkable and crazy idea until they saw the videos, but it was clearly apparent that the idea of going there didn't light her fire one bit!

* * * * * *

Sarah was making a good adjustment in working at Dr. Finch's pediatric clinic, which was conveniently located only a few blocks away from their home. She truly loved her work and working with Dr. Finch. She was also often able to keep TJ with her at the clinic while she was breast-feeding him, which made her job even more comfortable and convenient.

Tim's idea about their taking TJ to Belize was still making no sense at all to Sarah because she was a loving and highly protective mother who would jump off of a tall bridge or fight off an army before she would expose her precious little baby boy to anything that would be potentially dangerous or too uncomfortable for him.

Things were also doing well for Tim at Fort Bragg, where he was serving as a Brigade Medical Officer, working part-time at the Womack Army Medical Center as a psychiatric resident, and occasional part-time duty in Dr. Cason's psychiatric clinic in Fayetteville called the Raintree Clinic. Dr. Cason's private practice, called the Raintree Clinic, was managed by its staff psychologists, Dr. Ernie Gore, who was a former County Deputy Sheriff prior to earning his academic and professional credentials, and Dr. John Dickson, the Clinical Director. John, Ernie, and Tim worked well together and were becoming good friends.

Moreover, Ernie and John were also committed Christians, which added a special depth to their friendship. Ernie's and John's main functions in the clinic were to administer certain psychometric tests and provide therapeutic counseling for clients; especially for those with substance abuse and relationship problems who needed it after Tim had done the initial psychiatric assessments, prescribed appropriate medications, and developed medical treatment plans with them for some of their patients.

John and Ernie basically took charge of the day-to-day operations at the clinic except for the prescribing of psychotropic medications, which Tim usually took care of after normal hours. In his very little bit of free time, Tim just couldn't get his mind off of the Belize mission idea that Allen had proposed to him, and he had frequent enjoyable fantasies about Sarah and him going there.

Like Sarah, Tim also realized that the Belize mission wasn't practical and didn't fit well with their prior professional plans, but he felt a deep moral obligation to become involved and give needed help for the underprivileged in the church's mission there, even though it wouldn't be convenient or in his family's personal benefit to do so…and, most important, Sarah didn't appear to be the least bit interested, mainly because it would interfere with her mommy's role with TJ.

Chapter Thirteen

Sarah and Tim did finally agree that they would serve as members of the church's outreach mission medical committee at the church, but with the mutual understanding that their role in it would be limited to working from Dumont, mainly in helping to plan the medical part, and it would not be a commitment for them to actually physically go to the mission project in Belize to treat patients.

When they viewed the videos that had been sent to the church by Dr. Ben Gerardy and his wife, Dr. Mary Gerardy, who were the missionaries there, which showed the poor children and several adults who were in such bad physical shape, Tim felt such a deep compassion for them and wanted to get more involved with the operation of the clinic.

But, as much compassion as she also felt about the people there, especially for the little children, Sarah clearly wasn't the least bit interested in actually going there, no matter how hard Tim tried to persuade her to be.

He had tried every way he could think of to spark an interest in her to want to go there and help out, even for a couple of weeks out of the year, but Sarah wasn't about to leave their precious baby, TJ, for even a few days, much less for up to two weeks and possibly more, to go anywhere without him for any reason!

One afternoon, Tim locked the door to his office, got down on his knees and began to pray. *"My Lord and dearest friend, Jesus, You know how much I want Sarah and me to do the Belize thing and help out those poor people who need us, but she's not the least bit interested; so can you please suggest what I can do to motivate her to at least give it a try?"*

Tim paused and waited for the answer from Jesus, and it came quickly. *"Tim, you're making a big mistake in trying to expect Sarah to swallow the whole thing at once, and you should know by now that's not going to work. Remember that Sarah is first a woman and a mother, and they think differently from us guys...they are much more cautious and protective of their babies, as they should be.*

Instead, if you want to get her into the game, Tim, you should patiently feed the idea to her a little bit at the time, perhaps like suggesting a few days of vacation at a nice hotel in Belize for the two of you. While you're there, take her out for a short visit to the mission and once she meets the missionaries and the children I'm sure she'll become more interested and may decide to get on board with you and your dream to help those poor people of which I deeply approve. Good luck, buddy!"

When he returned home that evening, Tim suggested that they go out for dinner, which Sarah gladly accepted. They drove over to Fayetteville to dine at their favorite restaurant, The Hilltop House, along with little TJ, who was now being weaned from Sarah's breast milk.

As they were finishing their favorite dessert of Beth's famous carrot cake, which little TJ had spread all over his face until he was nearly orange, Tim said to Sarah that he understood that they've both been so darned busy and stressed since they finished their residencies and started their new jobs that he felt that the two of them ought to take themselves a little vacation break as soon as they could get away for a few days.

Tim said that he was pretty sure he could get a week's leave from the Army and thought that Dr. Finch could manage to get along without her for a few days.

He asked Sarah if she agreed and if she had any thoughts as to where she would like to go for some sorely needed relaxation time. Sarah replied, "I agree that a little vacation for us would be very nice and, no Honey, I don't have any strong thoughts about anywhere in particular, but a few days off from work and away from here to go anywhere would probably be a good and needed break for both of us.

Maybe we could shoot down to Tybee Island for a few days and stay at the great hotel that we enjoyed so much during our honeymoon. How about you? Where would you like for us to go?"

Tim said that he was thinking that they might do something really different for a change and, while he understood her feelings about not wanting to get too involved with the place, he'd like for them to slip down to Belize for just a few days, but only for some relaxation and fun.

They had been hearing so many positive things about it from Allen, and he told them he understood that they have some really nice beachfront resorts there that are pretty reasonable where they could chill out on the beach and pick up some sunrays for their milky-white skins and fool around a little.

He asked Sarah if that would interest her. Sarah frowned and said, "Hey, pal, I thought you wanted us to take a vacation to relax. If we were to go to Belize, then I'm sure you'll probably wind up hanging out and working at the church's mission the whole time, and that's not my idea of a real vacation…so please stop trying to finagle me into that mission idea because you should clearly know by now how I feel about that."

Tim told her he promised that if she agreed they wouldn't even go to the mission to work there at all; that they would spend no more than a part of a day out of the entire week there just so they could take a look at it and share what they find with Allen and the mission outreach committee at the church to help them with their planning when they returned.

He asked if she had any objections to their doing that. Sarah replied, "Okay, Honey, I'll go along with it, but only if you will absolutely promise me that it'll be no more than one day at the mission and the rest of the week we'll be relaxing and tanning ourselves on the beach. Also, only if it will be convenient for one of our parents to take care of TJ while we're away…but no longer than a week now. Do you give me your sacred promise on that?"

Tim wanted to jump and shout "Yippee" for this small but greatly welcomed baby step of success, but calmly smiled and told her that he promised it would be no more than a week and he would contact their close friend and travel agent, Anne Sternlicht, to make the arrangements for them to fly down to Belize in the coming month for a five-day vacation at one of their most famous and posh beach resorts.

When Anne's husband, Marty, who was a good friend of Tim's father and a fellow member of the Kiwanis Club, heard about their planned trip, he thoughtfully sent them a basket with a huge bottle of champagne, two throw-away cameras, and a large container of sun tan lotion to enjoy on their trip.

* * * * * *

After receiving an enthusiastic willingness from both Tim's and Sarah's parents for TJ to share staying with them, Sarah and Tim packed their bags and were driven by his parents to the Raleigh-Durham Airport for their trip south. They had made reservations to stay in a very fancy resort that was located on one of the Cayes (islands) on the Caribbean Sea off of the coast of Belize for five days, whose total cost, including airfare, was less than what a week's stay for them at nearby Myrtle Beach would be.

Tim was excited, knowing what his real secret motivation was, and Sarah was suspicious but hoping that it would only be a real vacation and not a sneaky trick on Tim's part just to draw her into involvement with the church's mission there.

They flew from the Raleigh-Durham Airport to Houston, Texas, where they changed planes for an American Airlines flight to Belize. Upon arriving in Belize City, they boarded a "puddle jumper" flight on a small aircraft over to nearby San Pedro, and then went by a water taxi to their final destination at a smaller island called Ambergris Caye. Once they arrived at Ambergris Caye, they were impressed with the beauty of the island and their very luxurious quarters which included a king-size bed in the large beachfront resort.

After they enjoyed a delicious dinner at the resort's gourmet restaurant, Sarah and Tim went for a nice moonlight walk along the beach; then returned to their room where they enjoyed sharing a bottle of champagne and happily engaging in their favorite mutual hobby of great lovemaking! Early the following morning, Tim and Sarah went out to the beautiful white sandy beach in front of the resort and enjoyed a great day of sunning, swimming, and relaxing.

On their third day, as they were stretched out on the white sandy beach and enjoying the sun, Tim leaned over to Sarah and asked her how would she feel about their taking a short run out to the mission the next day for just a few hours and take a look at it in the real, and not just on a video, so they could report back to Allen and the church outreach committee on what it's actually like when they returned home. Sarah smilingly replied to him, "I was wondering when you were going to get around to your real reason for our taking this otherwise fabulously enjoyable trip, Honey.

Okay, if it will make you happy, and that's the only reason I'd go there, then we'll do it…but only for one day and we will definitely not make any commitments to go back. Do we have ourselves an agreement, Sweetheart?"

Tim gladly agreed to her terms and then hugged her. They shook hands on it and Tim thanked her for her support and understanding. He then raced for the resort desk to make the travel arrangements to go by water taxi, about a two-hour ride, into Belize City and then rent a vehicle to drive out to the church's mission site which was in a small village located about thirty miles west of Belize City.

Early the next morning, they left Ambergris Caye by water taxi and were in Belize City a little before noon, and then leased a four-wheel drive Jeep for the trip out to the mission's location. After traveling cross-country over a rough and unpaved dirt road, they finally arrived at the facility where they were met by Drs. Ben and Mary Gerardy, who were the missionaries in charge of the mission's operation.

Ben Gerardy was a charming and hospitable gentleman in his early seventies who, with his lovely and much younger and very attractive wife, Mary, met Tim and Sarah at the gate to the mission's compound and warmly welcomed them into their residence, which was located in a small but attractive wooden building with a thatched roof.

Ben was a retired Disciples of Christ minister who had once held a high position as a Regional Minister in his church before retiring, one that was somewhat similar to that of a bishop in the Episcopal Church. Ben's lovely wife, Mary, who had been a college professor and vice president at a major university, had retired early when Ben was diagnosed with terminal cancer a couple of years before.

It was their mutual choice to spend what they then believed to be Ben's final months of life in this beautiful little country which they had previously visited and enjoyed while on a vacation there several years before.

While there, they saw how poor and in need of both spiritual and physical help so many of the inhabitants of their area were, and were deeply moved by it. They decided to do what they could to help them and started up the mission facility.

Ben and Allen Roberts had been long-term friends who had met when they were both students at Sewanee University, and that friendship is what led the St. Thomas church to become a major supporter of the mission project. Amazingly, since moving to Belize and starting up the mission, Ben's cancer had suddenly gone into a complete remission, and he became much healthier and fit than he had been in years. He was even going for a daily two-mile run with Mary!

His oncologist used one word to explain what had happened to Ben… miracle! Ben took Sarah and Tim on a tour around the small mission compound, which included a small ancient Mayan stone structure, a church, a school, and a large dining hall. Ben said, "It's so good to meet you guys and we really appreciate your dropping by. My old friend, Allen, said you would be dropping in on us and might be able to help by giving us a hand in starting up a medical clinic to help some of our poorer people who have no medical help at all."

Upon hearing that, Sarah suddenly froze up and felt somewhat annoyed because she sensed that Tim had planned this vacation thing all along only as a diversionary trick just to get her to get involved with him in the church mission, something to which she had previously expressed her strong feelings about their not becoming involved in other than in its planning part which was to be done only from their church in Dumont.

When they entered the mission's small chapel, a very cute little five-year-old girl named Millie rushed up to them and said, "Hi, Papa Ben. I just finished raking up the dirt floor in our chapel and I hope you and Jesus will like it." Sarah observed that the precious little girl's legs were covered with badly infected sores and scabs that appeared to be the result of many insect bites, and immediately felt compassion for her.

She held the little girl on her lap while she examined her and knew what treatment would help clear them up. She told Ben and Mary to wash her legs in some Clorox and water and she would get some better medications sent to them. Little Millie hugged Sarah and thanked her for helping her to get rid of her itchy bug bites.

Sarah was immediately hooked with feelings of affection towards this sweet and dear little child! Tim happily observed this warm interaction between Sarah and Millie, and silently thought to himself, Thank you, Jesus…looks like it's working just like You told me it would! It was an easy downhill run the rest of the way to motivate Sarah towards becoming involved in the mission after she had met and instantly fallen in love with Millie and several of the other little children there! The sun was beginning to set and Sarah and Tim had some trepidation about driving back to Belize City and then taking the long water taxi run back to the resort in the darkness of night.

When Ben and Mary invited them to stay with them for the evening, they gladly accepted. The Gerardy's treated them to a delicious fresh seafood dinner and, after they had finished eating, Tim complimented Mary for the super fare. Mary said, "

Thanks for your kind words, Tim, but Ben is the chef here. I do the administrative management stuff, try and help the disabled, and run the children's education program, but Ben's the chief cook and bottle washer on this team."

After their warm and interesting visit was over, Mary led Sarah and Tim to their quarters for the evening. Although the small guest room was clean and neat, it was a far cry from the luxurious suite they had been enjoying back at the resort on Ambergris Caye.

As they lay beside each other in the bed, Tim leaned over and asked

Sarah if she was angry with him for their longer than planned stay. He told her that he honestly didn't realize they would be staying there at the mission overnight…but told her that her positive reaction to everything that had happened there that day had exceeded his greatest hopes and he really did appreciate her attitude.

He asked Sarah if he was correct in assuming that she was beginning to feel a little bit more interested in the possibility of their helping out on this project. Sarah hugged him and said, "I'm not just a little bit interested, Honey, I'm really getting pretty excited about it and I'm looking forward to helping these poor little sweet children.

And I must give you full credit for being one heck of a slick salesman in tricking me into coming here because I never thought I'd feel this way about it. I just have to figure out how we can make this work with TJ, because I'd feel uncomfortable about exposing him to some of the unique diseases this area might have, which I'll have to check out. I'm still pondering over how we can make this happen, though, so please be patient with me and don't count me completely in or out of it quite yet!"

After enjoying a nice breakfast with Ben and Mary the following morning, Sarah and Tim drove back to Belize City and then took the long water taxi ride back to Ambergris Caye and their resort. They spent two more days basking in the luxury and comfort of the resort when Sarah surprised Tim by asking, "How would you feel about our going back and seeing Ben and Mary one more time before we catch the flight back home? I really liked them and want to see how little Millie's legs are doing.

I would also like to pick up some better medicine to give Ben and Mary to help the other children with infections like little Millie had until we can figure out a way to help them more." Tim smiled and quietly thought to himself, Thank You again, Jesus, for bringing my dear wife into the mission fold…I think we have her solidly hooked and in the boat with us! Early the next morning at the resort, Sarah and Tim packed their belongings and took the two-hour water taxi ride back to Belize City. After picking up a rental jeep, they dropped by a local drug store, loaded the Jeep with medical supplies and some personal gifts for Mary and Ben, and then headed out to the mission. After unloading the medical supplies and visiting with little Millie and some of the other children, they bade Ben and Mary farewell, promising to return soon, and prepared to head back to Belize City for their return flight home.

As they got into the jeep to leave, little Millie ran up to them and gave each of them a sweet hug and kiss goodbye, and pleaded with Tim and Sarah to come back and see her and her friends again as soon as they could. Sarah hugged her and said, "We'll be back, Sweetheart!"

This statement brought happy tears to Tim's eyes… Once they were buckled into their American Airlines seats on the plane headed from Belize City for Houston, Sarah gently put her hand on Tim's arm, adoringly looked at him through tear moistened eyes said, "Thank you, my dear husband, for showing me the right way for us to go.

I know it wasn't easy for you to deal with my selfish resistance to it, and you'll never know how deep my love is for you when you have the courage to stand up against my negativity for doing what we both know is the right thing for us to do as Christians. It's like Jesus said to you by 'walking the talk."

Tim told her not to thank him because it wasn't he who did it…it was Jesus working through both of them. Besides, they really liked Ben and Mary Gerardy a lot, and believed they were going to really have a great time in helping them out with their mission.

Chapter Fourteen

When their flight arrived at the Raleigh-Durham Airport Tim's Mom and Dad were there to meet them. They brought little TJ with them, and Sarah was beside herself with joy to see him.

She couldn't stop hugging and kissing the precious little fellow all the way home! On the ride back to Dumont, they filled Tim's parents in on the details of their experience in Belize and they were pleased to hear of Sarah's and Tim's decision to help support the church's mission there by getting more involved in it and by going on site…and not just because they would be helping others in need, but because Tim's Mom and Dad selfishly knew that would give them more enjoyable time alone with TJ! After stopping over and enjoying a nice family dinner at the Hilltop House, Sarah, TJ, and Tim were finally back home and, despite the enjoyable trip away, they couldn't have been happier to be back in their home which, compared with Ben and Mary's simple and small residence at the mission, was a palace!

Allen Roberts and his wife, Patty, had left Sarah and Tim a nice bottle of their favorite red wine, cabernet sauvignon, for them on their porch with a welcome home note attached. Tim called to thank them and told them that he and Sarah would be giving a full report on their Belize trip to the church's outreach missions committee at their next Sunday evening meeting.

They had also received e-mails from Mary and Ben Gerardy expressing their pleasure in meeting them and letting them know that little Millie's and several of the other children's skin sores were already nicely healing, thanks to Sarah's good medical advice, the gift of medical supplies; and, most of all, for their wonderful caring about the children.

When Sarah and Tim returned to their respective professional duties the next day, a ton of work had been awaiting them, and they had to spend nearly twelve straight hours a day in just taking care of urgent patients and the mound of paperwork that had accumulated during their short absence.

As Sarah was working with her relatively healthy young patients at the clinic, especially when she compared them with the general condition of the little children down in Belize, her thoughts kept going back to thinking of little Millie and the other needy children back in Belize and how much more serious medical help they needed. Tim was having the same thoughts while he was working with sick soldiers at Fort Bragg.

That evening, they were both bushed from doing all the catch-up work, but it wasn't nearly over for Sarah, the obsessive-compulsive homemaker that she was, so the McDonald's didn't get to bed until Sarah had finished bringing the home up to her high standards of operating room cleanliness at nearly midnight, at which time they crashed!

With their final words of the evening, they ended their usual nightly prayer with, "We pray the Lord our souls to take."

* * * * * *

When Sunday came, Sarah, TJ, and Tim went to the church where they were happily greeted by their families and many friends. Several people asked them questions about the trip to Belize, and Tim told them they would be giving a full report that evening at the outreach mission's committee meeting.

That evening, in what was ordinarily a relatively small group of no more than a dozen church members in attendance at the outreach mission's committee meetings in the past, the parish hall was nearly overflowing with people who were excited and interested in hearing reports from Sarah and Tim about their recent experiences in Belize.

After Reverend Roberts, who chaired the event, opened it with a prayer and a few words about the mission project, he introduced the program, and Sarah and Tim stepped up to the podium together.

Tim began by telling the group that he had always been aware and appreciative of the fact that Sarah and he have been two very blessed people…that they have enjoyed their comfortable home in Dumont; that he has been blessed with the best and smartest woman a man could ask for as a mate in his lovely and sweet wife, Sarah; a super little son in their little guy, TJ; loving and supportive parents and in-laws; their wonderful friends in this beautiful and comfortable church; their rewarding professional careers, and an overall highly satisfying and comfortable life for which they were deeply grateful.

He went on to tell them that just a little over a week before, he and Sarah had decided to visit the small country of Belize, which, as some of them may not know, was once a colony of the British Empire in Central America and is bordered by Mexico in the north, Honduras, to the south, and Guatemala to the west and sits on the beautiful Caribbean Sea.

It is also the only Central American country where English is the primary language, which appealed to them since neither of them knew a word of Spanish beyond Si.

He told them that he and Sarah had initially stayed in a very nice luxury resort on one of the country's beautiful islands, and enjoyed a fabulous time together basking in the sun and enjoying the beautiful climate there.

But on their third day when he and Sarah drove out to an extremely poor part of Belize this past week to visit the church's mission there, he became even more aware of and grateful for how well off they are, and how in their worst days here they are far better off than these poor people are on their best ones.

Tim said that most of us are prone to take a lot of things for granted in our very blessed lives here in the United States, despite our sometime crazy economic and often petty political issues. If we need water, all we have to do is turn the faucet handle and out it comes, hot or cold, rather than having to walk a long distance to a creek with a jug and carry unpurified water back to a home that's not nearly as nice as our outdoor storage shed, and we enjoy having two nice automobiles that we drive on nicely paved roads instead of having to walk nearly everywhere. "If it's too hot for us in our country, we simply flip on a switch and our homes here are cooled down; and if it's too cold, we just flip on another switch to make them warm up.

But that's not the way it is in many other parts of the world, and especially in the hinterlands of the little country of Belize where the living conditions aren't much better than they were in this country back in the seventeenth century."

He reported that they had the pleasure of spending some very rewarding time with the missionaries there, Drs. Ben and Mary Gerardy. Tim stated that they were pleased to share with the committee that these two wonderful Christian people are giving so much of themselves to help these needy people of Belize, and they deserve all the love and support the church can provide them in their devotion to obeying our Father's edict for us to help the less fortunate people in this world. He then said that he would like for the love of his life, his dear wife, Sarah, to share some of her perspectives on their experience.

He asked Sarah if she would care to say a few words. Sarah stood and said, "I agree with all that Tim has said to you about our experience in Belize. I must confess that I initially resisted Tim's request that we go out to the church's mission there because I didn't think we could possibly find the time to do what I believed had to be done there.

But that smooth-talking guy of mine finagled me into going out to the mission, and that's all it took to change my mind, as it now stands out in my mind as one of the more meaningful and rewarding experiences of my life. As Tim just stated, we have also always taken so many things for granted from having lived the comfortable life that we have enjoyed from living here in North Carolina all of our lives.

But when a sweet little five-year-old Belizian girl by the name of Millie sat on my lap, emaciated from hunger and covered with multiple painful ant and several other types of insect bite infections on her legs, things that I had been trained to easily diagnose and treat, something very special happened inside me.

I realized that she and many of the little children there needed something that I knew I could give them above and beyond just a few dollars. From that moment on, I realized that I had to do more than just write a check to support our mission there; Tim and I had to invest something more important than money…ourselves!

When we met Ben and Mary Gerardy, two very distinguished and kindly Christian people who are our missionaries there, I felt such a deep appreciation for what they were giving of themselves to help those poor people, and a lot of guilt for what I must confess I had initially tried to resist giving.

For those of you who are able to do so, I encourage you to become involved in this important project where we are definitely doing God's work. As my husband, Tim, often says, it's walking the talk.

We've placed quite a few photographs that were taken during our trip on the parish hall bulletin board and will be glad to answer any questions that you might have. Thank you." Everyone stood and applauded Sarah and Tim, and they then answered a plethora of questions about the mission.

* * * * * *

The following Monday, while Sarah and Tim were working in their respective clinics, each of them received a telephone call from Tim's mother inviting them and TJ to join them at their home for "a very important event tonight that you just won't want to miss." When Tim asked what it was about, she replied, "I can't tell you what it is beforehand because it would ruin the surprise…just be here around six and you will see for yourselves!"

They arrived at Tim's parents' home that evening at six, wondering what was so special and secretive that his mother didn't want to share it with them on the phone. As they pulled their car into Tim's parents' driveway, they were shocked to see the remains of Amelia's wheelchair sitting in the front yard, and it had been burned to a crisp, with only the frame and wire spokes of its wheels still recognizable!

When they asked what had happened, his mother told Tim and Sarah they had burned the wheelchair to celebrate what they were about to see. As Tim and Sarah were standing in the entry foyer of the home, they were shocked to see Amelia skipping down the stairs, unaided; then she proceeded to do a twirl around like a ballet dancer, then jumped up and clicked her heels together."

Sarah and Tim tearfully and happily hugged Amelia while Tim silently thought, Thank you, Lord Jesus.

You are truly a great man of your word! Amelia explained what had happened to her. She said she had been attending a therapy session at the neurology clinic when she suddenly felt a surge of energy come into her body that was unlike anything she had ever before experienced. She was delighted and said she felt an impulse to let go of her walker and spring out like a ballet dancer.

Her chief neurosurgeon, Dr. Bruce Jaufman, was so amazed and pleased to see her incredible and rapid recovery that he took a video of Amelia doing cartwheels to show off at his next professional medical conference.

She was, indeed, a walking miracle! During the same time period that she was recovering from her neurological issue, Amelia reported that her ophthalmologist, Dr. Wayne Riggins, had examined her vision and discovered that she was now 20/20 in both eyes, and there was no medical explanation for this sudden correction into perfect vision…a seeing miracle!

After everyone was seated in the living room, Amelia happily announced to the group, "I have some more good news that I wanted to share just with you all, the ones who have always stood beside me and given me your love and support during my difficult times and for all of my life."

Amelia was scheduled to receive her Bachelor of Science degree in Chemistry from Methodist University in the next month, with honors, and had applied to several medical schools, with her preferred choice being the highly respected and difficult to get acceptance into, the Duke University School of Medicine.

She proudly passed around her letter of acceptance into the Duke University School of Medicine, along with a sizeable scholarship she had been awarded, which everyone applauded as Amelia sat with a wide grin on her beautiful and very proud face.

She said that her goal was to become a neurosurgeon in the future so that she could help other young children who had experienced difficulties like she had suffered from for so long.

Tim excused himself and went into the bathroom. After locking the door, he fell to his knees, bowed his head and with tears of joy, silently said, Thank You, Jesus, my dearest friend in the world.

You are indeed even more of a man of Your word, and I promise to try, in every way I can, to do as You direct me to do, and keep on 'walking the talk'.

Tim returned to the living room and, after giving Amelia another warm congratulatory hug, he, Sarah, and TJ, left for home to enjoy a sorely needed restful night of sleep.

✱ ✱ ✱ ✱ ✱ ✱

Three weeks later, while working at the pediatric clinic, Sarah received a very unhappy telephone call from Ben Gerardy. "Sarah, I hate to be the bearer of such sad news, but I felt that you would want to know. It's about the little girl, Millie, who had become so attached to you while you and Tim were here; in fact, she would often refer to you all as her 'Aunt Sarah and Uncle Tim'.

The precious little girl passed away in her sleep last night after running a fever of nearly one hundred and four degrees for several days. She had been suffering from some kind of severe abdominal infection because she told us her tummy was hurting, but we didn't know what to do for her other than to give her some of the stomachache medicine you gave us.

We'll probably never know for sure what the cause of her death was since they don't do autopsies here. Little Millie's last conscious words to me were to ask me to call her Doctor Aunt Sarah and tell you that she loves you and will tell Jesus how good you and her Uncle Tim had been to her. We will be having her funeral here at the mission on the day after tomorrow and hope you and your wonderful husband might be able to join us on this sad occasion."

Upon hearing this unhappy news, Sarah's heart was crushed and she cried for nearly an hour before she was able to call and share it with Tim.

This brought tears to Tim's eyes as well, and he asked Sarah what she wanted to do. She tearfully replied, "Please make some flight reservations for us right now, Honey.

I don't care what the consequences are, but we must go to Belize as soon as possible because I can't let something awful like this ever happen to one of those precious little children again. If our parents aren't able to keep him, we'll even take TJ along with us if we need to."

Tim agreed, and called their good friend and travel agent, Anne Sternlicht, to make the reservations for a flight to Belize as soon as possible. Tim's and Sarah's parents were willing—enthusiastically so—to keep TJ, and Tim's commanding officer was kind enough to allow him to take the week off as did Dr. Finch for Sarah.

Tim's parents then drove them to the Raleigh Durham Airport. When their flight arrived in Belize City, Ben and Mary Gerardy were waiting for them at the airport. Mary tearfully said, "Millie's family and friends will be so pleased that you are honoring her by being here for her funeral, and Ben and I deeply thank you both so much for being here for her and for us at this very sad time for all of us."

Tim told Mary that as much as they shall all miss the little angel, they were certain that it was a great day for our precious little Millie when she would meet our Lord Jesus, whom he know has already had her on His lap and welcomed her into Heaven with open arms.

Mary agreed and thanked Tim for the uplifting comment. The four of them rode out to the mission in Ben's Jeep and the ride was even rougher than they remembered it as being during their previous visit.

When they arrived at the mission, several hundred of the local village people were gathered at the mission gate to welcome their honored guests from the United States. Ben, Mary, Sarah, and Tim then proceeded to the chapel, which was filled with local people, and the body of little Millie was laid out in front of the altar in a small open wooden casket.

When Sarah saw her lying there, still and cold, she couldn't help but to lean over and kiss little Millie's forehead, even though she realized that she could be risking exposing herself to a potentially dangerous infection by doing so.

When everyone was seated in the chapel, Ben began the funeral service for little Millie. "My dear brothers and sisters in Christ, today we are honoring the precious departed soul of our dear little Millie Smith, and giving our thanks to Him who gave little Millie to be with us during her brief stay here on Earth.

This precious child whom we will all miss is now in Heaven and making it an even happier place for all there with the presence of her spirited little soul. Even though we shall all miss her, let us not grieve, but we should instead rejoice that we had the pleasure of knowing our dear one; and she will be there, waiting to meet us when our life on this earth is over.

This little angel touched and was touched by so many people, especially our good friends who traveled here from the United States and had met her just a little over three weeks ago, and have now returned back to our mission to bid her goodbye.

Doctors Timothy and Sarah McDonald have touched all of us with their love, caring, and willingness to help us live healthier lives."

Ben, who had given over a thousand funeral sermons with the greatest of eloquence during his long ministerial career, became choked up and, with tears streaming down his face, had to conclude his heart felt sermon with the brief statement, "Little Millie's precious soul is now and shall always be with our dear Lord, Jesus, in Heaven." After the funeral service was over and the burial would be later that afternoon, the McDonald's and the Gerardy's shared a light lunch at Ben and Mary's home.

While they were sitting at the table, Sarah asked, "Ben, is there a chance that I can examine little Millie's body before she is buried? Although I'm not a pathologist, I would like to see if my examination might indicate the actual cause of her death. I have some ideas about what she died of, and would like to try and either confirm or refute them.

My main concern is that if she died of something that's contagious and the other children have been exposed to it, we need to find what it was and do whatever we can to protect the other children from becoming infected by it."

Mary asked Sarah what she thought that might have been the cause of Millie's death. Sarah replied, "On the surface, and based on the symptoms that Ben reported, it sounds like it was peritonitis that possibly resulted from a burst appendix, which wouldn't present a problem of contagiousness for the other children; however, if it was something else, we may have to do some tissue sample taking and send them off to a laboratory in the United States that can identify whatever it was that infected her so badly."

Tim had a thought, excused himself and went for a short walk outdoors. Once outside, he asked, Dear Jesus, I know this is an unusual request, but can You give us some help in determining the cause of little Millie's death? He paused and awaited an answer to his prayer.

It came quickly. "Tim, the precious child is here in Heaven with us and she's already established herself as one of our cutest little angels. Sarah is correct in her initial diagnosis of peritonitis, and there's no evidence of anything harmful that would be communicable to the other children."

Tim thanked Jesus for the information, which he privately shared with Sarah, and which she accepted without question. She then surprised him when she announced that she would like to set up a general medical screening of all the children in the mission before they returned home. Sarah then sent an email to Dr. Finch with a long list of supplies and equipment that were needed and asked that he have them immediately shipped to her at the mission by air express.

Dr. Finch was supportive of Sarah's plan and everything she requested arrived via air express in Belize City on the following day. Dr. Finch also told her to stay as long as she felt it was necessary to get the mission's medical care facility up and running. Tim's commanding officer and Dr. Cason were also supportive and gave him the same permission to stay as long as they were needed.

The Millie Smith Memorial Medical Clinic was now officially born! For the next four days, Sarah, Ben, Mary, and Tim worked nearly around the clock in examining all the children and many adults in the area.

Several children and some adults had medical problems which Sarah and Tim were able to treat and they were even able to make arrangements for one little girl with a cleft palate to be flown with her mother back to Raleigh where a local surgeon friend of theirs had volunteered to perform a surgical correction of the child's disfiguring problem.

Tim stayed in close touch with the church mission committee with daily email reports on what was happening, and the necessary financial and logistical support was provided for them.

Sarah and Tim also spoke with TJ via telephone on a daily basis and he seemed to be happy and safe with her and Tim's parents' in their home. Overall, everything seemed to be going swimmingly well at the mission.

Chapter Fifteen

On their last day in Belize, as Sarah and Tim were preparing to leave the mission for their return flight home from Belize City, Tim's cell phone rang. It was his mother and she was crying uncontrollably. Through sobbing tears she said, "Son, you and Sarah have got to come home right away. TJ fell into our swimming pool a couple of hours ago and he nearly drowned. He's in the hospital now and isn't doing well. Please come home as quickly as you can!"

Tim told her that they were leaving that day and asked her for more details about TJ's status. She replied, "The emergency room doctor, Dr. Hall, said that TJ is in a coma in the intensive care unit from nearly drowning.

Please hurry home, Son! I'm so sorry it happened. We had just left him playing in his sand box for a few minutes and he wandered into the pool area when we weren't looking and fell in. I'm so sorry, son, I really am, and I hope you can forgive me. Please pray for God to save him."

When Tim told Sarah what had happened, she went into hysterical screaming and crying. "My baby, my poor sweet little baby boy; please dear God don't let him die! Oh God, it's my fault for leaving him!" Tim tried to calm her but he was also having such mental anguish over the situation that he couldn't stop crying, either.

He called Dr. Hall who told him that he and the neurologist were working with little TJ, but sadly reported that things weren't looking very well for his recovery at that point.

After hearing this upsetting news, Tim prayed, Dear Jesus, please help us by saving our precious son, please. You've always been here for us and we need You now more than we ever have. Please… After a pause, Jesus responded. "Don't lose faith, Tim. Get home to him now and know that I also love him, and the doctors are doing the correct things to help him recover. Keep your chin up, pal…and this too shall pass." Ben and Mary rushed them to the Belize City Airport and they were able to catch an earlier flight back to Charlotte and a connection on to Fayetteville, where they were met at the airport by Tim's father.

He was long-faced and his swollen eyes made it obvious that he had also been crying hard. The three of them raced to the Cumberland County Regional Medical Center in a heavy downpour of rain, and took the elevator up to the pediatric intensive care unit. Drs. Hall and Finch met them in the hallway prior to entering into TJ's room and both were looking down in the face as well.

Dr. Hall said, "Tim, I'm so sorry to tell you that it's not looking very good for your little fellow at this point, but we're trying to bring him out of the coma as best we can."

When Sarah and Tim entered TJ's room, they saw him lying motionless in the crib. Upon seeing him, both Sarah and Tim began to cry. Then, to their startling and happy surprise, little TJ then suddenly sat up in the crib, reached out his arms, and tearfully asked, "Mommy and Daddy, where you been? Please hold me."

And hold him they did as they spilled buckets of tears of happiness all over themselves! Tim couldn't wait to give thanks to Jesus for yet another deeply appreciated miracle from God! After a thorough examination to ensure that TJ was totally recovered, Sarah, two-year-old TJ, and Tim left the hospital for home.

With Sarah's and Tim's concurrence, TJ slept in their bed between them through the night and for several nights to follow. They also hired a nanny to stay with TJ during the daytime while they were at work rather than risk leaving him with their parents, whose ages were reaching the point where Sarah and Tim were not comfortable about leaving him alone with them again, especially after the scary incident at their pool.

Their parents sadly understood. Sarah and Tim reported in for duty at their respective workplaces, and were swamped with patients and tons of paper work.

But as busy as they were, their hearts and minds were still back in

Belize. One evening at dinner, Sarah surprised Tim when, out of a clear blue sky, she announced, "Honey, I've had the Belize mission clinic on my mind so heavily and concluded that we just don't belong here as much as we once thought; instead, I feel that we should somehow arrange to be in Belize more often where we are so badly needed.

There are plenty of psychiatrists, pediatricians, and medical people of all callings here in our area, and the needs of the people here are nowhere near that which we've seen with those poor people in our trips to the mission who are struggling to stay alive.

What are your thoughts Honey?" Sarah's words left Tim nearly speechless! In his wildest of dreams, he never thought she would come anywhere as close to arriving at such a major level of commitment as that. He told her that he completely agreed with her that they should help them as much as they possibly could with brief visits, but asked if she was talking about going there and staying for a longer period of time. Sarah replied, "That's exactly what I'm talking about,

Honey, if that's what they need, I'm prepared for all three of us to go and stay at the mission for as long as they need us. I know it's not the practical or easy thing for us to do, but that's where my heart is now and I'd like to find a way to help those poor people like my precious little Millie." Tim told her he would have to give it more thought and research, and do some heavy duty praying over it.

The idea really did appeal to him as well, and he shared her view that it's a calling which he agreed would be very hard for them to refuse. But he wasn't sure if they would be able to handle the economic aspects of it, nor if his commander would be willing or able to support him on this by granting him any more leave time than he already had taken.

He also pointed out to her that, between the two of them, they were presently at almost a six-figure income; however, if they were to go and stay at the mission for too much time, their incomes could drop dramatically." Sarah replied, "It doesn't have to be all or none for us, does it? I mean can't we develop a plan for the structuring of the Millie Smith Medical Clinic from here?

Then we could see how many other MD's, PA's, CRNA's, RN's and

LPN's we might be able to persuade to volunteer a couple of weeks of their time out of the year and plan our own schedule there based on that. A good P.A. friend of mine at Fort Bragg who also attends our church, Tim Phillips, and his wife, Barbara, who are both highly qualified P.A.s, have already volunteered to spend a week out of their year there.

I'm sure that Ben and Mary will be able to manage the day-to-day administrative and logistical issues and the other wonderful work they've been doing, as they've handled them quite well for the past couple of years.

We can even provide them and some of the residents there with training on how to do some of the basic preventative medical tasks."

Tim told her that the idea made a lot of sense and he really did appreciate her enthusiastic attitude towards helping these poor people who needed them.

He suggested that they should think more about it; then put together the basics of their plan and present it to the mission committee at the church and get their feedback. Sarah and Tim took out a large tablet, ironically one of the same ones they had started to use over four years ago for the planning of their wedding that wound up creating the only serious quarrel in their relationship, and started writing.

They put together a list of the supplies, equipment, financial support, and potential volunteer fellow medical professionals that would be required to set up and operate the clinic in an efficient manner. Things were generally beginning to settle down with Sarah and Tim in doing the medical work in the Army and at her clinic, and coordinating the activities of the mission's clinic in Belize.

They had succeeded in getting several of their medical colleagues and friends to volunteer a week of their time each year so the clinic would have an M.D., Physician Assistant, Nurse Practitioner, or Registered Nurse present for at least a weekend out of every month at the Belize mission. Things couldn't have been looking better for the future of Ben and Mary's mission!

* * * * * *

Tim's Army unit, the 505th Infantry Regiment of the 82nd Airborne Division, was scheduled to conduct a large airborne operation at the end of the month on Fort Bragg's Sicily North and Nijmegen Drop Zones, and Tim would be making his first parachute jump since finishing his basic airborne training, referred to in Army slang as his "cherry jump."

He was a little uptight about it, as most new parachutists are on such occasions, but wasn't overly concerned; however, Sarah's anxiety over his safety was about to go through the roof!

She later told him that she had been so worried that she was torn between the irrational idea of putting something in his food to make him ill on the scheduled day of the jump so he would be unable to participate in the operation, and actually going out and watching the operation along with Tim's proud parents. Fortunately, Sarah opted for the latter.

On the morning of the scheduled large airborne training exercise, Tim crawled out of the bed at four a.m., put on his Army gear and prepared to leave home for Fort Bragg and the pre-airborne operation preparations. Sarah tearfully pleaded with him to not go which, of course, he told her he must and that she needn't worry about him.

Tim told her that he would be okay as the serious injury rate in these kinds of things is far less than it is for people just walking across the street, so he asked her to please stop her unnecessary worrying about him.

He told her that he would be jumping from a C-130 aircraft which, according to the briefing he had received earlier, would be the seventh aircraft in the line formation, and would have a tail number of 4806J.

He added that he would be the third paratrooper out of the plane, would be jumping from the starboard side, and would wave at her with a large red handkerchief after his parachute was fully deployed. Sarah forced a smile and kissed him goodbye; then after Tim left, she sat on the toilet with anxiety-induced diarrhea for nearly an hour! *

* * * * *

Tim's Mom and Dad arrived at Tim and Sarah's home early that morning to drive Sarah and TJ with them out to the drop zone to watch the event, which was scheduled to occur at noon. On the ride out to Fort Bragg, Tim's father explained the details of how everything would take place and his enthusiastic pride for Tim's maintaining the family's airborne tradition was obvious.

He described for Sarah and Ruth everything that would take place. Tim would be issued a main parachute and a reserve parachute; then he would put both of them on and enter into the aircraft in stick order. "What is a stick, Dad?" Sarah asked. John replied, "A stick is a line of paratroopers.

There will be two of them, one on each side of the airplane, and each stick will be jumping out of the door of the aircraft on their side when they're ordered to by the jumpmaster.

Then the aircraft takes off. Once they are a few miles from the drop zone, a red light will appear over the exit doors and the jumpmaster will signal for all of the men to stand up. He'll then order them to hook up their main parachutes to a steel cable that runs along most of the length of the airplane.

After checking their equipment and that of the man in front of them, they'll let the jumpmaster know that they're ready to go. Then the first man will stand in the door and when the red light turns to green the jumpmaster will shout "Go" and they will jump out in turn.

That's about all there is to it, Sarah." Sarah anxiously asked, "What could go wrong, Dad? Like is there any way that Tim could be hurt? I'm so afraid for him." John laughed and said, "We'll be exposed to a lot more danger sitting in the bleachers and watching things where we could fall through the bleacher boards and break our legs or be hit by a bolt of lightning than Tim will be by jumping from the airplane, so please stop worrying your sweet self, Honey. He's going to be just fine."

* * * * * *

The C-130 aircraft carrying Tim and the other thirty-eight parachutists on board was passing the final ground checkpoint of a location known as Little River. The red light in the door turned on and the jumpmaster shouted, "Stand up!" The thirty-eight other parachutists on the plane and Tim then arose and faced towards the rear of the aircraft.

The jumpmaster then shouted, "Hook up!" at which time each of the men snapped a hook leading from their main parachute on to a steel cable.

He then shouted "Check Equipment!" and each of them made a visual inspection of what they could of their reserve parachute and that of the main parachute of the man in front of them. "Sound off for equipment check" shouted the jumpmaster, then each of the men tapped the rear of the man in front of them and shouted out that their number was okay.

Tim was feeling a little anxious, as this was his first jump since completing his basic airborne training several months ago, and he would be the third man in the stick to exit from the aircraft.

The jumpmaster then shouted, "Stand in the door," and the first man positioned himself in the open door. The red light turned off and the green light then lit up and the jumpmaster shouted, "Go!" and the men began to exit the aircraft out of the two doors on each side of the aircraft.

When Tim reached the door, he was tense, but swallowed real hard and leaped out of the aircraft…then something went very wrong and his main parachute became twisted and failed to completely deploy.

As he was rapidly falling, spinning, and barely slowed by his partially deployed parachute, he reached down and pulled the handle to activate his reserve chute and it deployed…but it then wrapped around his partially open main chute, causing his fast rate of descent to continue.

He was falling at a rapid rate and quickly hit the ground hard on his back, initially rendering him completely unconscious.

As he was being lifted onto a stretcher by the medics, he began to regain consciousness. The pain in his back was excruciating, and the medics carefully carried him to an awaiting ambulance.

As he was being taken by the ambulance to the Womack Army Hospital, Sarah, TJ, and Tim's parents, who had witnessed the entire disaster, then raced to their car, and followed behind the ambulance with tears in their eyes while they rode and said prayers for Tim's survival.

When the ambulance arrived at the emergency room of the Womack Army Hospital, Tim was rushed to the operating room where an orthopedic and neurosurgeon were on standby to receive him.

Sarah and Tim's family anxiously sat in the waiting room for a report on his status. Because of her M.D. qualification, Sarah had been invited to come into the operating room to observe

Tim's being treated if she wished to, but she declined the invitation as she said that she couldn't bear to see Tim suffering again. Emotionally, this was almost a replay of their Savannah experience of only a few years ago. After a couple of hours had passed, the neurosurgeon and an orthopedic surgeon came out of the operating room and explained the situation to Sarah. "Your husband is conscious now and is going to be generally okay after the multiple fractures in his spinal column heal and he gets some rehab treatment; but I'm afraid his military days may be over, as I don't think he could risk another trauma to his spine.

More than likely, it's going to result in his being medically discharged from the Army."

Sarah understood the situation from a medical and intellectual perspective; but emotionally she was nearly ripped to shreds! Among the more practical things, she was concerned as to the effect that this discharge would have on Tim's nearly completed psychiatric residency. His superior medical officer reassured her that, as far as he was concerned, Tim had more than satisfied him of his competency and said he would endorse him for the Psychiatric Board certification.

When Tim was finally rolled out of the operating room, Sarah and the family greeted him with kisses and tears of relief. Despite his pretty severe physical pain, Tim put on a smile and shared with her that he had heard from Jesus again, and that they would soon be pleased with the ultimate outcome of what then had first seemed to be a major crisis and setback to their plans.

Chapter Sixteen

After spending nearly three weeks in the hospital recuperating from his injuries, Tim was finally released from the Womack Army Medical Center and allowed to return home for further recuperation. The Army had begun processing him for a medical disability retirement, for which he would receive a little over one-half of his basic pay and full medical coverage for him and his family for the remainder of his life. Also, after he passed the Board's written examination, which would be no problem for Tim, he would become certified as a psychiatrist.

What he and Sarah had initially perceived as a major tragedy and setback in their lives had become somewhat of a blessing in a way, by providing them with more flexible options, especially regarding their missionary plans.

Over the past several months, Sarah and Tim had experienced so many traumas in their personal lives, and decided that they needed to have a "date night" where they could be alone and privately enjoy each other's company with a little romance and discuss their future professional career options as a result of Tim's recently changed military status.

After enjoying a delicious dinner at the Hilltop House, Sarah said, "You know, we've really got to get our arms back around the Belize mission situation, Honey, because we've not even spoken with the committee or with Ben and Mary since we got back from there a couple of months ago and we've had far too much on our plates to handle in our own personal life. How would you feel about our taking a quick weekend trip down there to assess and update ourselves on the situation before we make any more plans?"

Tim told her that was amazing, because he was thinking the very same thing, and would give Mary and Ben a call to see if they would like them to come down there for a short visit in a few weeks and give them a hand. Tim dialed the Gerardy's phone number on his cell phone and Mary answered. When she realized that it was Tim calling her, she suddenly began to cry and said, "I'm so glad you called, Tim, because I was planning on calling you in the morning.

Ben and I received some horrible news a few weeks ago that you would want to know about. You may recall that Ben's cancer had gone into what appeared to be a complete remission just a couple of years ago, and he's been healthier than ever since then.

Well, he hadn't been feeling very well for the past several weeks and he suddenly rapidly began losing weight, so we decided to take a flight up to Miami, Florida to get him checked out by a doctor there. To make a long story short, after examining him for two days, the oncologist discovered that Ben's cancer had suddenly come back in a rage and had quickly metastasized all over his body again, and it's even worse than it was the last time. It looks like I could lose him any day."

Tim expressed his sorrow in hearing that and told Mary that Sarah and he would catch the first possible flight out and come down to be with her and Ben right away if she would like. Mary replied in a choking voice, "That would be so wonderful of you and Sarah, Tim, and I know Ben will also be happy to see you both."

After the phone call was over, Tim explained the situation about Ben to Sarah. They then shared a prayer, seeking God's intercession to help Ben and Mary cope with their tragic situation; then called Anne Sternlicht, and asked her to make the quickest possible flight arrangements to Belize for them.

A few minutes later, Anne called back and said she was able to get them a flight out early the next afternoon. They also decided they would take TJ, who was a few weeks from turning three, with them on the trip this time.

After the harrowing experience they had when they left him behind a little over two months ago with Tim's parents, although they in no way blamed them, Tim and Sarah didn't want to be apart from their son again.

Tim called Reverend Roberts the morning before they left for Belize, and filled him in on the situation so he could update the church's mission committee.

* * * * * *

When they arrived in Belize City, Mary met the McDonald's at the airport. She told them she had to make the drive by herself because Ben's strength had dropped to the point where he was barely able to even stand up, much less drive, or even leave their home.

On the ride back to the mission, Mary explained what had been happening since Tim and Sarah had last been there, with the most significant item being Ben's sudden rapidly failing health.

She said, "I hope and pray that Ben will recover from this, Tim and Sarah, but it's not looking very likely according to his doctors. If it's God's will that Ben should soon join Him in Heaven, I will definitely want to try and stay on with the mission, and whatever support you dear friends and your wonderful church will be able to provide us will be deeply appreciated."

Tim reassured her that they were with her all the way, regardless of Ben's outcome. After the rough and bumpy ride from Belize City, they arrived at the mission.

When they entered the Gerardy's home, they were saddened to see that Ben had experienced a sudden and substantial loss of weight, and was so weak that he couldn't stand and was barely able to speak…yet he still wore the warm smile on his face that he always had.

After a few minutes, Tim excused himself and went outside. He leaned against a tree and prayed, Dear Jesus, my very best friend and savior, please share Your plan for our friend, Ben, with me, if You will, and tell me what You would have us do to help with the mission situation.

Jesus replied to Tim, "It's time for our friend, Ben, to come home, Tim. He's done a wonderful job as one of my very best ministers for a long time and has certainly more than earned the right to join us here. He will be leaving you all shortly, and I would like for you and Sarah to help Mary pick up the pieces and continue the mission work that she and Ben started."

Tim realized that he and Sarah now had no decision to make because his best friend, Jesus, had already made it for them.

When he returned from a long meditative walk, he found Sarah hugging Mary, with both in tears. Mary said in a choking voice, "my best friend and soul mate has just left us to join our Lord, and I'm so happy for him.

I'm sure going to miss him, but he's earned the right to go into the next life and I know we'll be there together again one day."

* * * * * *

Ben's funeral was held four days later and there were so many people there to say their goodbyes to him that the service had to be held outdoors instead of in the tiny mission chapel.

Allen Roberts and his lovely wife, Patty, had flown in for the service at which he officiated, as did several members of the church's mission committee. There was a seemingly endless line of people who waited for the opportunity to eulogize Ben, and the stories they told were beautiful.

No national president was ever given more kudos than Ben for the many contributions he had made to humankind! A dear friend and key lay leader of the church that he once served as its pastor in his Fayetteville, North Carolina days, ninety-five-year-old Eleanor Manning, made the flight to honor him. As always, Eleanor was beautiful, perky, bright, and with a great sense of humor, and she gave one of the most beautiful and touching eulogies they had ever heard.

A couple of days after all of the funeral activities were over, Tim, Sarah, Mary, Allen, Patty, Eleanor, and Tim sat at a table together and discussed the future of the mission, with special emphasis on the medical support it required and who would provide it.

They also decided to name the mission "Camp Bennett" in Ben's honor and memory. Mary made the commitment to remain at the mission for the remainder of her life and her oldest daughter, a registered nurse, committed to working with the team for a week out of every other month.

Sarah and Tim had previously decided that they were also going to continue making the mission their primary purpose in life, possibly by even relocating to Belize as their permanent home if it became necessary.

They arrived back in Dumont and, after giving it several days of thoughtful and prayerful consideration, Sarah and Tim made the most major decision of their lives…that if they were really sincere about their commitment to walk in His steps, they would have to give up all they had in Fayetteville and return to Belize to help serve God's children who were there and needed them.

After Tim and Sarah made the major decision, they liquidated all of their major tangible assets, including the sale of their Dumont home; planned to take the money and build themselves a home that would fit in with the Belize environment, home school TJ, and make the best of the situation by enthusiastically doing the work for which He had called them to do.

* * * * * *

After his long reflections of things of the past were over, Tim looked up into the sky, gave a smiling salute to Jesus, and went back inside their home for the last time. He needed to get some rest since he, Sarah, and TJ would be leaving in the morning for the Raleigh-Durham Airport to catch a flight to their new home in Belize and continue their walk in His footsteps.

Tim's Experienced Based Thoughts From His Taking The Walk

Most of us have committed regrettable errors in our past by not doing many things we should have done and by doing many things we should not have done, and most of these actions and inactions have to do in our relationships with others. Unfortunately, we cannot simply rewind the tape of our past negative and incorrect behaviors of the past toward others, erase them from our minds, and go on as though they never happened.

We must acknowledge and atone for them where possible, seek the forgiveness of God and whomever we offended, and move forward on a better path, the one laid out for us by Jesus. The areas over which we must apply important changes to our behavior are on the road that lies ahead in this life, regardless of how many or how few miles we have left to travel on it.

My **ABC**'s for living and enjoying the good life are:

Always avoid Anger because you cause yourself and the person towards whom you feel it unnecessary pain, and most of what we do or say while in a state of anger is destructive to everyone concerned. Do not succumb to Anxiety, as your living in fear of bad things that might happen interferes with your ability to appreciate the real things that are happening around you, and Arrogance, which prevents you from enjoying mutually rewarding relationships with others.

Be *Benevolent*, and always mindful of the importance of sharing your Blessings with others who are less fortunate, especially those who are in need of your love and caring, and seeing the Beauty and good that exists in others rather than their faults.

Care about how others feel, and seek to handle relationships by following the wisdom and guidance given us by **Christ** and doing unto others as you would have them do unto you; and be quick to extend your forgiveness of them if they have hurt you.

On the remaining part of our journey through life, if we walk the talk of God in our lives, true happiness and our greatest dreams will come true, and most of them will last forever!

What is the "talk?" The talk is contained in God's Word (aka the Holy Bible), in the moral compass that is built into our psyches (described by Dr. Sigmund Freud as the superego), following the ways in which we are told by Him that we should live by carefully listening to the educational and inspiring sermons presented to us by ministers, priests, and rabbis in our places of worship, and through our daily communications with Him through prayer.

These steps will serve to produce all we need to ensure that our walk stays acceptable, positive, and on track, and that our souls will land safely in the next and eternal phase of life after our temporary lives on Earth come to an end. Then, the essence of our being, our souls, will be taken by God and we will live forever!!!

In His Service,

www.ingramcontent.com/pod-product-compliance
Lightning Source LLC
Chambersburg PA
CBHW071404120626
46546CB00002B/800